imagine...

To Joe & Milly

Best friends!

Jack &
Anne

Jacob D. Eppinga

Jacob D Eppinga

October - '00

CRC Publications
Grand Rapids, Michigan

Imagine . . . © 1997, CRC Publications, 2850 Kalamazoo Ave. SE,
Grand Rapids, MI 49560.

Cover photo: ©Tony Stone Images

ISBN 1-56212-323-8

10 9 8 7 6 5 4 3 2 1

contents

Preface 5

1 Imagination 7
2 Perspective 11
3 December Dream 15
4 When I Became an Orphan .19
5 An Old Story in Modern (Un)dress 23
6 Divine Mix 27
7 Dream in the Morning, Angel's Warning 31
8 Trees 35
9 Creativity 39
10 The Far Country 43
11 The Choice 47
12 Revolving Doors 51
13 The Chandeliers 55
14 Jesus Is Coming to Town 59
15 Of Body and Soul 63
16 Dreams 67
17 Guide for Church Hoppers .71
18 The Sweeper 75
19 The Sting 79
20 Of Mice and Men 83
21 Family Troubles 87
22 Chain Reaction 91
23 Spare Tire 95
24 Sef 99
25 Christmas Tree 103
26 Push! Push! 107

27 Yummie 111
28 A Modern Yankee in Solomon's Court 115
29 Bon Appetit 119
30 Space Trilogy for Advent 123
31 Nothing Sacred 127
32 Keeping Up 131
33 Fabrication 135
34 Exegesis 139
35 Forgive Us 143
36 The Daze of Our Years 147
37 The Blahs....................................151
38 The Circle of Our Discontent 155
39 Oscar 159
40 Versions 163
41 Any Room? 167
42 True Story...................................171
43 An Easter Sermon 175
44 I Am Joe's Soul 179
45 Selective Hearing 183
46 Mutual Admiration Society 187

preface

Imagine . . . Imagine that! Just imagine! Can you imagine?
These are daily expressions. We hear them all the time.

To imagine is to image something in your mind. People who say they can't do this kind of "imaging" are said to have no imagination. Children generally have imagination in spades. Imagination gives life to the dolls and trucks they play with. When they are afraid of the dark, it is because their imaginations are running overtime: shadows become bogeymen. Their "imaging" can run wild when they are in the attic or the basement all alone. Sounds become sinister. But when they're with friends in the same attic or basement, they can spend hours playing church or cops and robbers or dressing up in Mom's old clothes and pretending. Imagination again.

Psychiatrist Carl Jung said that without fantasies no creative work would ever come to birth and that, therefore, the debt we owe to imagination is incalculable. True! Novels, plays, poetry, paintings, symphonies—all these find their genesis in the human ability to imagine. Television can dull this gift. That's why plays on radio are better than TV, and novels better than both. They activate our imaginations.

James Thurber, in *The Secret Life of Walter Mitty*, wrote about a man standing outside a store. He was waiting for his wife who was shopping inside. Boredom set in. So, standing there, he daydreamed. He was a sea captain mastering a storm. He was a man bravely facing a firing squad. Et cetera. It was imagination that relieved the tedium.

In Handel's *Messiah*, the baritone dramatically sings the words of Psalm 2. "Why do the people imagine a vain thing?"

Alas, they often do. And what about the words of Genesis 8:21? "For the imagination of a man's heart is evil from his youth" (KJV). Again, alas! Sin has touched everything. Even our imaginations.

But imagination can be used for good. Jesus' parables use imaginative ways of helping us see and understand the kingdom of God. And in Mark 8:1-10, we have a wonderful picture of Jesus imagining the plight of those who followed him, and who, on their homeward way, might suffer from lack of food. How wonderful if we would employ our imaginations in a similar way, placing ourselves in the shoes of the lost, the hungry, the imprisoned, the poor, the fatherless, as he did. Then we would be moved, as Jesus was, to help others.

In the first verse of the Bible, we are told that in the beginning God created the heavens and the earth. Look around! Before he created all things, he imagined all things. What an imagination!

We are in his image. We can imagine too.

But enough. The pieces that follow are all connected, in one way or another, with imagination. So, sit back, relax, and—

Imagine . . .

imagination

Chapter One

I flew high in the air recently on a magic flying carpet. When I mentioned this to a small friend of mine who is in the sixth grade, he took issue with me. He said it was no carpet; it was a 747. Magic had nothing to do with it. Flying is a matter of aerodynamics.

What a shame! Science may be great, but it is robbing our children of their wonderful, God-given imagination.

Not long ago I taught a few classes in story writing at Ada (Michigan) Christian School. To write stories, you need imagination. I couldn't very well talk about it without giving the children an illustration. While I was sitting at home trying to dream one up, the squirrel with no tail ran past my window. He's been hanging around our house for the past year.

What a sorry sight! He's about as happy with his situation, I suppose, as those three mice who had their tails cut off for

7

chasing after the farmer's wife. Other squirrels cavort on our lawn in pairs and chase each other up and down trees, but my squirrel without a tail is always alone. The way he walks shows the sadness that has invaded his life. I decided to make him the subject of my story.

Once upon a time, there was a squirrel without what is beyond a doubt the pride and joy of every squirrel: a tail. In his presence, other squirrels waved their own tails unnecessarily, making him feel his loss all the more. Feeling constantly shunned, he decided to move away and live somewhere in solitude.

When he came to the corner of the street where he lived, he met a zebra without stripes who looked about as sad as he did without a tail. They talked, and each told the other his troubles, which were the same: nobody would have anything to do with them. The zebra without stripes had an idea. "There must be others like us," he said, "so why don't we build a home together and make it a haven for peculiar animals?"

The squirrel without a tail agreed, and soon the house was completed. They lived there together happily. One day there was a knock on the door. It was a bird. She wanted to know whether the home for peculiar animals had room for a bird. She said she had acrophobia, a fear of heights. The other birds always poked fun at her for keeping her feet on the ground. The squirrel with no tail sympathetically let her in.

The next day came another knock on the door. It was a fish, flopping on the doormat. He wanted to know whether the home for peculiar animals had room for a fish who absolutely hated water. He called his fear *aquaphobia.* "But you can't live without water," said the squirrel with no tail. The fish said that nowadays people were inventing substitutes for everything, so why couldn't animals invent a substitute for water? So the zebra without stripes, who was very inventive, came up with a substitute, and the fish moved in with the others.

The neighborhood animals quickly became aware of the home for peculiar animals. They didn't want it in their neighborhood. Among other things, it was against something called "zoning laws." They appealed to the king. King Lion agreed and promised that later that night he would lead a raid and destroy the home for peculiar animals. When the zebra without stripes heard about this, he quietly took his scissors and, finding the king snoozing in the sun, cut off his mane. When King Lion woke up to lead his forces against the home for peculiar animals, everybody laughed and poked fun at him. He looked funny without his mane, so they would have nothing to do with him.

That night there was a knock on the door of the home for peculiar animals. The squirrel without a tail and the zebra without stripes and the bird with acrophobia and the fish with aquaphobia all answered the door. When they opened it, there stood the king without his mane.

"May I come in?" he begged. They let him in, and they all lived happily ever after.

This story, admittedly, is not in a class with Hans Christian Andersen. If it has to have a moral, it might be that animals don't do these things to other animals, but people do—to other people. In any case, children at Ada Christian School—and children everywhere—hold on to your sense of imagination and develop it. It's one of God's great gifts to you. Too many grown-ups don't have it anymore.

And the next time you see a 747 in the sky, remember that it's a magic flying carpet.

perspective

Chapter Two

I am a four-year-old. The minister must be about a hundred. I am sitting next to Daddy. Mommy is in the nursery with my little sister. Pretty soon, when everybody sings, us kids will get up and go downstairs to church school. I like to swing my legs, but Daddy won't let me. He sits real still. All the grown-ups sit real still. Like they're dead, almost.

The minister knows a lot—even more than my father. The minister is talking softly now, but sometimes when we kids are downstairs, we can hear him hollering. I wonder why. Is he mad?

The lady in front of me has a big neck.

I have a quarter in my pocket for church school. I wonder what God would do to me if I kept it. The minister just said that we must not covet. I wonder what that means. Must be something bad.

I am a twelve-year-old. The minister is preaching. The little kids have all been sent downstairs for children's church. The pews seem a lot emptier. I remember when I used to go downstairs. That was ages and ages ago.

I hear a noise behind me. I wonder what it is. I would turn around and look, but my parents would not approve. They say turning around in church is bad manners.

The Tigers are losing too many games. They made some dumb trades last winter. I've got some baseball cards with me. Maybe I can make some good trades with them in church school class after church. We're studying the Heidelberg Catechism, and I don't know my lesson hardly at all. Dad usually checks up on me, but either he was too busy or just plain forgot to ask me the questions. Here's one: *What is Providence?* "Providence is that activity of God whereby he upholds . . ." Oh no—I forgot! Hope we don't have a test this week.

My teacher, sitting on the other side of the aisle, is our high school principal. He knows a lot. I think he knows more than the preacher. But the preacher is OK. I like to listen to him, especially when he tells stories. I get kind of lost when he uses big words, though. Last week he talked about Jonah. That was good. A month ago he talked to me after church. He said he hoped I would make profession of faith soon. None of the other kids do it when they are twelve, so I won't either. I'm too young. But I do love Jesus.

I am an eighteen-year-old. I was up late last night and wouldn't have minded sleeping in this morning. But my folks wouldn't stand for that. Some of my friends may be sleeping in, though. I don't see them here this morning.

The minister is kind of boring. To tell you the truth, I don't know what he's preaching about right now. They could do something to liven things up around here. Sing some different songs, maybe. Get some action going. The preacher could be a lot more dramatic too.

Hey! Who's that girl across the aisle? I never saw her before. She's nice looking—maybe I can meet her after church. It's hard to get to know people here. After church, everybody stands around with their own little clique. What am I supposed to do?

I am a thirty-year-old. With four children to get ready for church, no wonder I'm out of breath by the time I get here. I hope my children sit still today. Last week they were awful.

Did I turn the burner off on the stove before we left this morning? Maybe I should write a note to my husband and hand it to him when he comes by to take the collection. He could go home and check the stove. Wouldn't it be awful if the usher got my note instead of my husband and brought it to the preacher? What would he think if he read, "Go home and turn off the gas." He might take it personally. He wouldn't deserve it because he's a good man.

I hope the children let me listen this morning. I get something from the sermon when I listen.

I am a sixty-seven-year-old. The minister seems so young! But he's a good man. I pray for him every day.

It makes me feel good to see so many children in church. Young people too. Families are sitting together. I remember when our boys were small and my late husband would lead us all down the aisle. That seems like only yesterday.

I wonder what the future will be for that little four-year-old who is swinging her legs. I wonder what it will be for that twelve-year-old who is sneaking looks into his book. I wonder what will happen to that teen who is looking at that girl across the aisle.

Say! That mother must have had quite a time getting her kids all dressed so nice and off to church on time. I remember how busy Sunday mornings were when I had my family. What blessed days those were.

Here we are, young and old, to worship God. Thank you, Lord. Bless the pastor's message and apply it to every heart. Amen.

december dream

Chapter Three

Funny how things can get so mixed up in dreams.

A long and busy day had left me drained and desperate for rest. As sometimes happens when one is overly tired, however, my sleeping hours were as disturbed as my waking hours had been. A telephone jangled somewhere in my dream, ringing hollowly and endlessly as I struggled toward it with heavy feet. A distant voice asked whether I would make a hospital call.

"It's a young woman," the caller said. "She's had a baby, and I wish you would visit her tonight."

Strange that such a call was so urgent. Her name was "Mary" somebody. I wrote it down on a piece of paper. She was not a member of my congregation nor of my denomination. She was not Protestant. She was not Roman Catholic. Instead, I discovered that she was a member of some synagogue a considerable distance away, in another city. "So why me?" I wondered, as I put on my shirt, somewhat weary in the service of the Lord.

The hospital was the most unlikely place I had ever seen. Though it was night, many people milled around. And the lobby was an absolute disgrace. Instead of comfortable chairs and tables spread with reading material, mules and goats and cows wandered around! Picking my way gingerly among them, I came upon a man wearing a nametag. "Keeper," it read. "In," said a sign on the desk where he sat. Well, obviously, he wasn't "out."

"You'll have to go to the admission office," he said, "though, of course, at this hour it is closed." Assuring him rather icily that if I needed such a place, I would certainly choose one roomier and cleaner, I fished for my piece of paper and asked to be directed to Mary's room.

"You will find her in the ward," the keeper said. "Probably not wealthy enough," I thought, "to afford a private room."

I found her easily. She was a quiet person. Though she responded very little, she listened eagerly when I read an Old Testament psalm. She seemed to be pondering in her heart all that I read. When I left, I suspected that her spiritual roots were deeper than my own.

On my way out I passed the nursery, crude as the lobby, where many people were gathered. I recognized a few of them. There stood, of all people, King Hussein of Jordan, King Abdul Sa'ud of Saudi Arabia, and Nur Al Din of Syria. The poor surroundings accentuated the elegance of their dress. I gathered from their conversation that the gift they would leave with the young mother would more than meet the hospital bill.

These eastern notables were not the only visitors. I met some sheep ranchers from Australia and New Zealand. An elderly man from a local rest home, a nurse said, had been coming daily for a year. This venerable gentleman made a little speech, which some attributed to a bit of hardening of the arteries. He said he could die now because his old eyes had seen salvation.

On my way out I met the office manager. He seemed excited about the baby; he found the mother such a saintly person that he said he was going to propose naming the hospital after her.

Outside, I drew a deep breath of fresh air. Across the street a cluster of men and women stood looking up into the sky. Joining them and following their gaze, I heard the man next to me say that what they were looking at was a space craft, maybe a satellite in orbit. But others disagreed. They claimed that what they saw looked more like a special star.

It was all too much for me. Instead of going home, I headed for my church to sit and reflect. In the eerie light of breaking dawn, the birds flitting around the steeple looked more like tiny angels. I watched them for a brief moment when, suddenly, the tower chimes began to play. The tune was familiar: "Joy to the World."

The noise awakened me.

Funny how things can get so mixed up in dreams! It wasn't real, of course. It really didn't happen. All except that baby.

He really did happen—two thousand years ago.

when i became
an orphan

Chapter Four

It was the year of the great stock market crash. Charles Lindbergh was courting and marrying Anne Morrow. The fabulous Babe Ruth was leading both leagues with a batting average of .404. Al Capone was going to prison. And we were going to Europe.

Father sat proudly behind the wheel of our brand-new Hupmobile, and I occupied the navigator's seat, with my little three-year-old brother between us. Mother, in the back, cared for the twins, who were still in diapers and who were hollering a lot. We were driving from Detroit, Michigan, to Hoboken, New Jersey, where we would board the *Volendam*. It would carry us—car and all—to Rotterdam.

Undertaking such a journey with four boys, two of whom were not yet housebroken, must have been a daunting task. Indeed, there were a few moments when Mother wanted to call the whole thing off. But our steamer trunks had already been shipped ahead. And anyway, as Father explained, Mother would get some occasional relief: at age twelve, I was a built-in baby-sitter.

Triple-A cards guided us to our destination. They bore instructions such as "Three miles past Toledo, turn left at the yellow house." The cards led us to a place called Delaware Water Gap, where Father found a large room above a café to house all of us for the night. After putting my brothers to bed, Mother, looking the worse for wear, went downstairs with Father for a break and a cup of coffee.

They left me in charge. "We'll be back soon," Father said. There I sat, in the dark, by a window, looking at the lights of a strange town. It was 9:00 P.M.

My parents never returned. It was well past midnight when I finally went downstairs to the café and told the manager. I noticed that our car was gone. The police came. My brothers had awakened and were crying. So was I. The next day a stern-looking woman with a big black hat took us to an orphanage. I told her where we lived in Detroit, and that we had no grand-parents, uncles, or aunts, except in Europe. I gave her the name of our minister.

After several days in the orphanage, our minister and his wife came to take us back to Detroit, where we were divided up among the church members. The newspapers printed lots of stories about us. My brothers were better off than I was. In the house where I lived, I received beatings with a strap—some-times for nothing at all. That's why, when I saw my chance, I ran away, taking my brothers with me. I sailed away on a raft in the Detroit River. Like Tom Sawyer. But I was very sad.

At 9:30 P.M. my parents came back upstairs. My inner despair turned to deep joy as my father's voice broke my solemn reverie. "Anything happen? Everything all right?"

"Nothing happened," I said nonchalantly, even though in the space of a half hour, so much had happened that had not happened. What a comforting sound it was, an hour later, to hear my father snoring. I felt snug and secure.

Mother was seasick from the moment we left port. Father and I and little brother roamed the decks. It was great fun! But the large cabin that held us all was a place of gloom. Everywhere, clotheslines held millions of diapers trying to dry. Mother, weak and wan, felt comfortable only when lying down. She said she wanted to die.

Father had a different idea. He took her up and outside for fresh air. It would do her good. "We'll be back soon," Father said. There I sat. I was in charge. My brothers' diapers hung down everywhere like church banners. It was 3:00 P.M.

My parents never returned. They had both jumped overboard. When we arrived in Rotterdam, we were divided up among the relatives. Like all Dutch kids, I had to wear short pants. People put their hands on my head and said, "*Arme jonge*" (poor boy).

At 3:30 P.M. my parents returned. I leapt from sadness to gladness. After one whiff of our cabin, however, Mother went back to her bunk.

Was I an insecure child? I don't think so. My parents were wonderful—none better. I think, though, that sometimes imagination can be stronger than a sense of security. I thought of all this when I read about those parents who went vacationing in Mexico while leaving their small children alone at home.

Children of the heavenly Father also imagine sometimes that he has forsaken them. They should remember what he said: "Never will I leave you; never will I forsake you" (Heb. 13:5).

an old story in modern (un)dress
with apologies to Hans Christian Andersen

Chapter Five

An Old Story

Once upon a time lived some rogues who posed as weavers. They promised the emperor, always fond of new clothes, to make him a most wonderful garment. Its colors and patterns would be more realistic than any he had ever seen. Furthermore, the materials would bear the unusual property of being visible only to the sophisticates, remaining invisible to all who were unfit or extraordinarily simple in character. The emperor agreed and thus, being rogues, they pretended to weave.

The emperor sent his faithful old minister to preview the work of the weavers. But the faithful old minister saw nothing whatsoever. Only empty looms. Believing the lie that only the worthy could see the materials, he was greatly shaken. Was he a simpleton? He could see nothing at all, no matter how he strained his sight. But not wishing his wisdom and worthiness to be questioned, and unwilling to risk his job, he reported to the emperor that the garments were indeed exciting to the eye.

The emperor sent others to inspect as well. They too saw nothing. Yet they too, not wanting to be considered unfit, reported that the garment in the making was both supercolossal and terrific. Finally, the emperor went himself. Seeing nothing, he was greatly discomfited. Apparently, he alone was unworthy and simple, for all others sang the praises of what eluded him. Unwilling to reveal himself as a simpleton, he too praised the work of the rogues.

When the pretended garment was completed, the pretending weavers pretended to dress the emperor for the premier parade down the broad way so that all the citizens could see. But all the citizens saw was their emperor in the nude. Wishing, like everyone else, to appear knowledgeable and wise, all praised the beautiful colors and patterns of the emperor's new clothes. All, that is, except some children. They could see nothing but an old man with no clothes walking down the broad way. Being unsophisticated and innocent, they told their elders that all they saw was a naked man.

In Modern (Un)dress

Once upon a time lived some rogues who posed as moviemakers. They promised the people, always fond of films, to produce some new and most wonderful creations clothed with patterns of such significance and socially redeeming qualities as had never before been seen. Furthermore, they said, their materials would separate the men from the boys, in that those who saw nothing in their productions would reveal themselves unsophisticated and ignorant. Only the socially aware and progressive would be able to discern and see. And so, being rogues, they pretended to weave their great cinematic finery.

The people sent a faithful critic to preview the work of the moviemakers in order that they might read a review. But the faithful critic saw nothing at all of what was being trumpeted as both significant and socially redeeming. Believing, however, the falsehood advertised by the rogues that only the sophisticates and progressives would understand and see and, furthermore, not relishing being labeled unsophisticated, he reported to the people that the cinematic efforts he had seen were, indeed, intriguing to the eye. And soul.

The people sent other critics, but they too saw nothing. But not wanting to be considered uncultured and dull, they reported in the entertainment pages of the newspapers that what they saw was both supercolossal and terrific. All of this, of course, heightened the expectancy of the people who could not wait to see the great productions, which were clothed with significance and dressed in the dress of socially redeeming qualities.

The great premier opened on the broad way where all the citizens could see. But none saw the apparel of significance, and none saw the dress of socially redeeming qualities in which the films were supposedly arrayed. All for the simple reason that they did not exist. What the people saw was dressed scantily in underwear and less. Afraid to speak the truth, however, and thus risking being considered unsophisticated, all praised the beautiful cinematic significance and socially redeeming qualities. Even some of their churches and church publications joined the praises, for they too did not wish to be considered backward. Only the children took exception. Being unsophisticated and innocent, they said that all they saw was a bunch of naked people.

Contrary to popular opinion in this empty age, there is sometimes nothing more in the "reel" world than meets the eye.

divine mix

Chapter Six

It was the coffee hour after morning worship. Cup in hand, I drifted from group to group, picking up snatches of conversation on a wide range of subjects. My sermon seemed forgotten in favor of the latest news and the scores of the previous day's sporting events.

The one exception was headed in my direction. He was older than most of the others. I gathered from his expression that he had been sucking a lemon. He said something about some confounded kids. They had sat in front of him. They had taken away the blessing. He had heard nothing of the sermon. He didn't come right out and say it, but his further observations implied he'd be a lot happier, and we'd all be a lot better off, without the young ones around.

Suddenly, it seemed as though time stood still. In the space of the next second, I had a daymare. (Sometimes daymares can be more frightening than nightmares.) In it, I saw a world bereft of children and their toys, schools, and playgrounds. All people had simply appeared on the scene fully grown. They seemed to have sprung forth from the foreheads of the gods, as in ancient mythology.

Old men didn't go fishing with grandsons, for they had no grandsons. Old women couldn't relive their girlhood days, for they couldn't look into the eyes of nonexistent granddaughters. The divorce rate escalated as some husbands and wives drifted into flat relationships unseasoned with sons, daughters, nephews, and nieces.

Even Christmas, its true significance undiminished, somehow lacked luster in the absence of the little ones, with church school programs and new toys lighting up their faces. Businesses failed without young men and women moving up the ladders with new ideas. Every day the world more resembled an old people's home in which the three great virtues of faith, hope, and love seemed strangely diminished.

I shook myself back to reality. Acknowledging the remarks of the man with the lemon in his mouth, I made my way to my young people's class. I paused momentarily at the nursery door. Passing it before and hearing the wailing, I had always been thankful that all I had to do was preach. Nurseries somehow seemed beyond my capabilities. But now I breathed a quick prayer of thanks for all children.

In my classroom, however, the young people were up in arms. The elders had rejected their perfectly reasonable request for an evening pizza service. What was I going to do about it? One young man, in the full wisdom of all his thirteen years, declared that they would all be better off if the old folks shoved off.

Suddenly, time stood still again. In the space of the next second, I had another daymare. In it, I saw a world bereft of adults. The whole earth was a giant playpen. Pandemonium reigned supreme. It was the world of King Rehoboam all over again—the one who rejected his older advisers in favor of the younger ones and thereby split a kingdom.

Only this was even worse! The fifth commandment was suddenly rendered obsolete, for no one had parents to obey. None could learn, for there was none to teach. Nor was there anyone to caution, comfort, and advise. And who would provide for the needs of body and soul?

Again, I shook myself back to reality. I told the class about a young man who, at the age of fifteen, considered his father the essence of stupidity. He was surprised, when he reached his twenty-first birthday, to discover how much his father had learned in those intervening years. I said that perhaps they too, in a few years, would come to appreciate the wisdom of their elders.

Driving home afterward, I thought of the infinite greatness of the Creator. He thought into being a humanity in which not only the sexes but also the ages of the people complemented each other. He intermingled the young and the old. It's a nice arrangement: a mixture invented by God in which, in his church and by his Holy Spirit, the sons and daughters prophesy, the young men see visions, and the old men dream dreams (Acts 2:17). Old Paul and young Timothy—what a combination!

What a pity, then, when churches have age gaps. True covenant theology, applied, will neither ignore its young nor put its aged on the shelf.

dream in the morning, angel's warning*

Chapter Seven

In my dream I found myself in a great hall overflowing with all manner of creatures—some human, some not.

I was among delegations of leprechauns, elves, mermaids, children, animals, and not a few humans of various weights and measures. I sat between a professor of philosophy and an owl. It was a meeting of sorts.

The chairman was an egghead by the name of Humpty. Humpty, whose last name was Dumpty, leaned on a crutch and rubbed his bandaged head. Mr. Owl, to my left, whispered that Mr. Dumpty had suffered a great fall. Even so, he was well enough to lead the meeting.

*From *Mother Goose's Rhymes.*

The philosopher, to my right, explained that we were assembled to consider a movement to alter Mother Goose's nursery rhymes. He said he wasn't sure if he agreed with the last speaker, who had said that some of the rhymes dated back to the time of Henry VIII.

Mr. Owl overheard the philosopher. He leaned forward and, fixing his large eyes on the learned man, said that many of the rhymes existed even before old Henry VIII. His father had told him so!

They both ignored me and launched into an animated debate about Mother Goose's identity. Mr. Owl argued that Mother Goose was the Queen of Sheba. The philosopher thought that theory was difficult to substantiate. More likely, she was Charlemagne's mother or Robert the Pious's wife or, perhaps, Elizabeth Foster Goose of Charleston and Boston.

The noisy exchange between Mr. Owl and the philosopher drowned out what Mr. Dumpty was saying, so I changed my seat, moving next to a chicken. She said her name was Little. She kept eyeing the ceiling as if it might fall.

Ms. Little asked me if I was in the nursery rhymes. I said I wasn't. She admitted she wanted to be in them but didn't qualify. The rhymes had to come from an anonymous source, be of oral transmission, have the nature of a jingle, be short, and preferably have a lulling effect on little children.

She pointed out that most of those in the rhymes were seated in the reserved section, down front. I looked and recognized little Tommy Tucker, the ten o'clock scholar, Mary and her little lamb, Old King Cole, and many others. Mr. Dumpty rapped for attention and gave the floor to a revisionist who was seeking to alter the rhymes.

The revisionist, nattily attired, had a reddish complexion, a Mephistophelian beard, and horns. His tail lay neatly over his left arm, like a napkin carried by a waiter in a restaurant.

He delivered what I thought was an effective speech, making three points. First, he said, some of the rhymes needed correction. Cows don't jump over moons. It's impossible! And people don't normally head uphill to fetch pails of water. Nor do babies sleep in treetops. And pickled peppers are processed items and, therefore, can't be picked.

Second, continued the speaker, some of the rhymes needed cleaning up. A dish running away with a spoon is suggestive. Putting a thumb in a pie is unsanitary, as is Jack Sprat or anybody else who licks a platter clean.

And should Old King Cole smoke a pipe when tobacco is unhealthy? Isn't it immoral for mice to chase farmers' wives, to say nothing of the blood and violence involved in the amputation of their tails? And did anybody know that the rhyme of the king in his counting house was a chant used by the ancient Druids to choose human sacrifices?

The hall fell sober and silent. The speaker continued. In the third place, he said, the rhymes needed to be far more sensitive. Rhymes about poverty—ones that mentioned bare cupboards and simple Simons who couldn't pay pie-men even a penny—had to go.

The speaker sat down amid a great stir. Then the cat, who had emerged from the well to attend the meeting, hissed. And a certain Jack, whose head was patched with vinegar and brown paper, said that the rhymes had to be preserved because they would contribute immeasurably to the future culture of the nation.

I woke up. Too soon. How would it all turn out? "How silly," I thought. Myths, nonsense rhymes, and jingles are never in jeopardy. Only truth. Mother Goose is never in danger. But the Bible always is.

trees

Chapter Eight

Hi! I'm a tree!

Surprised? William Shakespeare, in *Macbeth,* says that trees have been known to speak. He forgot to add that we trees can write as well (besides providing the paper on which to do it).

I guard a golf course a short distance west of Grand Rapids, Michigan. I'm just to the left of the fourth fairway.

Every summer, a pitiful excuse for a golfer comes by almost weekly, spraying golf balls in all directions. Because I can't duck, I'd rather he went elsewhere. He has hit me countless times, yet he never apologizes. He does, however, sometimes speak to me. He once told me that he is a preacher and that he writes stuff about cabbages and kings and imaginations. I said that if he did that as poorly as he played golf, he ought to quit. I also suggested that he write about trees instead of cabbages for a change, but he didn't answer.

The last time we talked, he insulted me. He bragged that he had been to the Rock of Gibraltar and a whole lot of other places, and he pointed out that I hadn't moved an inch. I answered that there was something to be said for standing still if the alternative was to be blown about by every wind of doctrine—like a lot of cabbages and kings these days.

Trees, like people, come in all shapes and sizes. Our personalities, too, differ as much as human personalities. If the birch is the most shy and ladylike of trees, as James Russell Lowell once wrote, then the willow (the most messy) is the most unladylike. Even so, we all have our admirers.

I think that I shall never see
A poem lovely as a tree. . . .
Poems are made by fools like me.
But only God can make a tree.

Joyce Kilmer sold himself and all poets short with these lines. But what a nice thing to say about us trees! Ogden Nash was almost as flattering (and most unflattering to you) when he wrote:

I think that I shall never see
A billboard lovely as a tree.
Indeed, unless the billboards fall,
I'll never see a tree at all.

Robert Frost is another friend of trees. He wrote of the tree outside his window, "Let there never be curtain drawn between you and me." How delightful! Did you know that in the past, some people worshiped trees? "O Tannenbaum, O Tannenbaum," they sang.

Speaking of religion, have you ever noticed how large a part we trees play in the gospel story? Both paradise lost and regained feature trees of life. Eve ate of the fruit of the tree of the knowledge of good and evil. When the Savior came, Zacchaeus climbed a tree to see him. Jesus pointed to one of us as he taught a lesson about being fruitful. Later they hung Jesus on a tree. One of us held him when he died.

People often turn to us for lessons. Alexander Pope wrote, "As the twig is bent, the tree's inclined." How often don't people look at their offspring and observe how the apple never falls far from the tree? And did you ever stop to think about what we have in common?

We are both known by our fruits!

But let me get to the point. Would you plant one of me this spring? I have many enemies: wind, ice, lightning (fire), disease, insects, and humanity! True, some of you are my friends. But so many others have swung the ax needlessly. Meanwhile, I have always supplied you with food, shelter, and clothing. While beautifying your landscapes, my leaves have purified your air by breathing in carbon dioxide and breathing out health-giving oxygen. So would you plant one of me this spring? In a wooded glen in Upper Michigan, you can read my plea to you:

I am the heat of your hearth on the cold winter nights, the friendly shade screening you from the summer sun, and my fruits are refreshing draughts, quenching your thirst as you journey on. I am the beam that holds your house, the board of your table, the bed on which you lie, and the timber that builds your boat. I am the handle of your hoe, the door of your homestead, the wood of your cradle, and the shell of your coffin. I am the bread of kindness and the flower of beauty. Ye who pass by, listen to my prayer—harm me not.

creativity

Chapter Nine

A Calvin Theological Seminary professor was once caught going to the movies. This cost him his job. Years later, I became his pastor. When he was old and hard of hearing, the professor often haunted the streets late at night. Seeing him hoofing and hatless one frigid February evening, I pulled over to the curb and invited him to climb aboard. "I don't want your brains to freeze," I said. "Why don't you get a hat?"

He declined a lift with thanks. "My brains need cooling off," he said.

B. K. Kuiper was truly a character. I did not doubt that his brains needed cooling off because, even at an advanced age, the wheels in his head could not only turn, but spin. I recall a number of conversations in which that mind would spin miles ahead of me. In one conversation, Kuiper referred to a subject I always avoided—his dismissal from professorial ranks for the sin of entering a theater. (Incidentally, whoever saw him and blabbed did our church a great disservice.) Kuiper's observation, which he offered dryly and in passing, was that Christian Reformed people were now comfortably enjoying, on television, the movie that caused his fall from grace.

As an educator, Kuiper was fascinated with film and television as a potential teaching tool. Had he lived, he would have been equally captivated by videocassettes. Puffing on a cigar one day, he told me what films he would produce if he had a good movie camera. I smiled. He was all thumbs when it came to gadgets. I remember what he did one day to my sermon tape. I had come to his house to collect the tape and found yards and yards of it all over his living room floor, trailing into the kitchen. The reel had unraveled in his two left hands.

I am like B. K. in my love-hate relationship with gadgets, such as my video camera and VCR. I can't make the dumb things work the way they should. I dutifully carry our camera on our travels, but I find it easy not to buy any film. It's not only easier that way, but cheaper! You can take more pictures too! The fact is, I have an aversion to all such equipment. This does not mean that I have no ideas about what I would do with all this stuff—if I could.

Orson Wells and Ernie Kovacs were creative giants in the film world. Kovacs especially had an eye for life's vignettes and foibles. I have sometimes dreamed of being a kind of Christian Reformed Ernie Kovacs. That would take another lifetime, and I have only one. But I can dream a little.

I would like to create a short video depicting a wedding. In it would be a preacher, a bride and groom, and a congregation. Picture the scene: The minister reads piously from a bookstore catalog (or the Constitution of the United States or some recipes—anything but the wedding formulary). The bride wears a Carmen Miranda hat, a huge basketlike affair piled high with fruit. Everyone looks serious. The minister interrupts his reading to ask the groom whether he takes this woman to be his wife. The groom replies that he murdered his grandmother. The minister beams and asks the bride a similar question. She offers some abracadabra. The camera cuts to the closing scene, a triumphal recessional in which everybody is smiling.

In my dream, I distribute this cassette to Christian Reformed program committees that are looking for material. They use it for a discussion starter, asking questions such as *Does it matter what anybody says at a wedding? Who listens? Is what the bride wears more important than what she says?* Maybe such a cassette would provide the gentle sting some people need to get back to meaning and away from fashion parades.

Years ago, an animated cartoon taught me something. A man came home from work. He was tired and wanted to sit in his chair to rest. But in the chair sat a big letter *A*. It didn't belong there, so the man threw it out the door. When he returned to his chair, he found the *A* again. He flushed the letter down the toilet and returned to his chair, where the *A* met him again. He cut the letter into little pieces. He buried it. He locked it in an attic trunk. But no matter what he did, he found the *A* each time he returned to his chair. In desperation, he burned the letter in the yard and scattered the ashes. This time he was truly rid of it.

The man was exhausted! He dragged himself to his chair. But he could not sit in it. Occupying his chair was a great big letter *B*.

What a conversation starter this film could be! It prompts questions such as *What does it mean? Is life just one thing after another? Do these endless trials come from God or from someone else? Do "we wrestle, endlessly, with principalities, against the powers, against the world rulers of this present darkness, against spiritual hosts of wickedness in the heavenly places"?*

The Lord has given us great tools. Will some among us—young people, perhaps—use them in clever and stimulating ways for the cause of our Lord?

the far country

Chapter Ten

January: *Dear A.B.,* I'm glad you landed such a good job. Find a good evangelical church in your new area and attach yourself to it. I was one of the first people you looked up when you moved to our city, even though we were strangers then. Soon after, you made profession of faith, remember? Now that you have moved away, I'm sure you will want again what you sought when you came here—a good church. With Christian greetings, your pastor.

January: *Dear Pastor,* So good of you to write. I miss our church most of all. Say hello to all my friends in the Young Adults Group. Heard Dr. P. Piper last Sunday. He plays a strange tune. Can't really tell you what he preached about, but it wasn't from the Bible. Will do a little church hopping till I find something of which you'll approve and where I can feel at home. Your friend in Christ, A.B.

March: *Dear A.B.,* The Young Adults Group really misses you. Surely do appreciate the leadership you gave it. We'd all like to see you back here again. But we can't all be in one place, can we? God in his providence scatters us, I think, so he can have witnesses everywhere. Remember to be one. Found a good church yet? With Christian greetings, your pastor.

June: *Dear A.B.,* I look forward to seeing you on your vacation, if you can make it back as you planned. Did you get my last letter? I am eager to hear about the church you are attending. I hope too that by this time you have found some good Christian friends in Big Town. With Christian greetings, your pastor.

September: *Dear Pastor,* Sorry I couldn't make it back this past summer. As a matter of fact, I didn't get to see my folks either. By the way, I'm still attending that church I mentioned to you, mainly, I guess, because of a girl who attends. She's great. Wish you could hear us talking. She's got some different ideas. She believes all religions are really parts of each other. Your friend, A.B.

November: *Dear Pastor,* We are worried. Our son, who was by you until last January, isn't writing to us as frequently as he did at first. This we can understand, for he has a busy life. It is what he wrote in his last letter that is disturbing. He seems to be thinking ideas he never had before, especially in religious matters. My wife and I, we have prayed about this. And we thought we'd write you because you understand these things better than we do and because maybe, if you would write him about his spiritual life, he would take it from you more than from us. Thank you. The parents of A.B.

November: *Dear Colleague,* I have a member in Big Town, about seventy miles from you. If you have time, I wish you would look him up. I enclose the address. I'm concerned for his spiritual welfare. I think it is a case of new surroundings, new people, and success competing with his commitment to Christ.

We'd be happy to pay your expenses. With Christian greetings, your colleague.

November: *Dear Pastor,* I had a visit from your friend. My fiancée happened to be present too when he called. She thinks that he has some pretty narrow views. I agree. The way I see it, there's room for both yours and Dr. Piper's points of view. A man gets a broader perspective when he gets out into the world. Your friend was a nice enough guy, but I can't say I appreciated his visit all that much. Look, Pastor, don't worry about it! A.B.

December: *Dear A.B.,* Sorry you didn't appreciate my friend's visit. My concern is with the ideas you expressed in your last letter. In this Christmas season, think about John 3:16. Surely, out of many, only one point of view on the Christ Child squares with this most wonderful Bible verse. Agree? With Christian greetings, your pastor.

April: *Dear A.B.,* Since Christmas I have written several times and wish you would reply. In this Easter season, I hope you can rejoice with all of us over a risen, living, victorious Savior. I commend you to him. With Christian greetings, your pastor.

May: *Dear Members of the Church Board:* This is to inform you that A.B. affiliated with us here at the Church of the Dead Savior, Big Town, at our Easter service last month. With Christian greetings, Dr. P. Piper.

May: *Dear Lord,* We pray for your prodigal children who have wandered to the far country, removed from you. Lead them to your side again. And may we as brothers and sisters pray for them each day.

the choice

Chapter Eleven

He was in prison and on trial for killing several people in cold blood. But after the sentence, which pronounced him guilty, the people wanted to set him free.

A large segment of the population grew vocal. Some erected enormous signs in the streets demanding his release, claiming extenuating circumstances. Bumper stickers expressed similar views. An avalanche of requests descended on the country's leader, demanding the prisoner's freedom. The whole land was in an uproar.

The jurors who had found the prisoner guilty were confused. They had done their duty. A prosecutor had presented incontrovertible evidence, and they had reached the only possible verdict. A helpless cleric had lost half his face; a child had been flung into a gutter; old men, women, and children had been herded into a ditch and slaughtered. What other conclusion could the jurors have reached, they thought, sworn as they were to uphold justice? And yet, despite their adherence to duty, the public was intimidating them, and vicious notes, anonymously written, threatened their lives.

Many leaders added their voices and supported the prisoner. Among them were those who had, heretofore, strongly advocated law and order. Yet now they too demanded a reversal of the verdict. True, not all prominent men and women were of this mind. The strange alchemy had not affected them all. Among them was one who said that the overwhelming public support for the guilty one defied justice. Another complained that the national conscience was more warped than he had believed possible. And some school children composed a letter expressing their fear of growing up in a country where murderers walked free.

But these were in the minority. The public reaction overwhelmingly supported the convicted one. Someone wrote a song that cast him as a hero. The prisoner received a mountain of mail, as many as ten thousand pieces in one day. He could not read them all, nor respond to them all alone. Good thing he had a secretary.

The clergy too raised their voices, mostly in the prisoner's support. One said that he must be acquitted; if he was guilty, then "so are we." Another opined that punishing one for what others had taught him was unfair. Still another labeled the verdict as "scapegoating."

Above all this din, in a difficult position, stood the country's leader. He couldn't ignore the unprecedented wave of public opinion. The prosecutor sent him a note, respectful yet forthright. The latter pointed out that unarmed and unresisting people had been killed. It was shocking! But the leader's intervention, equally shocking, compromised a fundamental principle of a civilized society. His observations were as indignant as they were eloquent.

The hubbub subsided somewhat, though it did not cease. The prisoner's name would be remembered. In the aftermath of the hot controversy, people sat around in small groups, talking of little else. One said, "It shows you that if all the people get together and make enough noise, you can get through to the top." Another said, "Too bad that in a situation like this, something, or someone, always gets crucified."

* * * * * * *

Oh, yes. I forgot to tell you the prisoner's name.
Barabbas!

With one voice they cried out, "Away with this man! Release Barabbas to us!" (Luke 23:18).

revolving doors

Chapter Twelve

Mr. A was Christian Reformed. Born and bred. His father had been a perennial elder; his grandfather, a minister who once served as the president of the Christian Reformed synod. Mr. A had gone to Christian schools. He had married into a Christian Reformed minister's family.

Yet he and his wife had become increasingly disenchanted with the quarrels in their church. The theological debates never ended, so they began to look around. After a few years, their feeling of alienation led them from First Christian Reformed Church to the Independent Bible Church.

They said they were happy there. Soon after they were welcomed, they read in the Sunday bulletin of their new church that Mr. and Mrs. B had recently transferred their membership to the local Presbyterian church. Mr. and Mrs. B were people of musical taste. The choir in the Presbyterian church was right up their alley. They had grown tired of choruses, keyboards, and guitars. The preludes, postludes, offertories, and choir anthems in their new church all had musical integrity. The worship was more liturgical. It was quite a step to take, but Mr. and Mrs. B took it—from Independent Bible Church to Knox Presbyterian Church. They said they were happy there. Soon after they were welcomed, they read in the Sunday bulletin of their new church that Ms. C had recently left to join the Roman Catholic church across town. She had finally yielded to her boyfriend's persistence and agreed to be married by his priest after taking instructions in the Roman Catholic faith. This was better, she thought, than having a house divided. Everyone agreed. And so she took the step. From Knox Presbyterian to St. Mary's Roman Catholic Church.

She said she was happy there. Soon after she was welcomed, she read in the Sunday bulletin of her new church that Mr. D, a son of St. Mary's parish, had moved to another city and had joined the Episcopal Church. Mr. D was an up-and-coming young man. His company had moved him to another state. His new town had no Roman Catholic church, so he tried a Lutheran church but liked the Episcopal church better. His new boss was also an Episcopalian and was pleased that Mr. D joined his church. And so Mr. D moved—from St. Mary's Roman Catholic Church to St. Luke's Episcopal Church.

He said he was happy there. Soon after he was welcomed, he read in the Sunday bulletin of his new church that Mr. and Mrs. E, who had been members of St. Luke's, had joined the Pentecostal church down the street. They had grown a bit tired of the Prayer Book and Episcopalian formality. They liked the freewheeling style of the charismatics and the dynamic manner of the preacher, qualities that suited their temperaments much better. And so they moved. From St. Luke's Episcopal to Maranatha Pentecostal.

They said they were happy there. Soon after they were welcomed, they read in the Sunday bulletin of their new church that Mr. and Mrs. F had left Maranatha Pentecostal to join the Christian Reformed church located a small distance out of town. It was a lot closer to where they lived, and furthermore, several of their friends went there. And so they moved. From Maranatha Pentecostal to Second Christian Reformed Church.

There they reared their children, all three of whom, in time, moved away. The older son moved to the city to work. Attracted by its aggressive youth program, he joined Central Methodist. The younger son went to the university. Through the campus chaplain, a Lutheran, he became a member of St. Paul's Lutheran Church. The daughter landed a job as music director at Mt. Zion Baptist Church downtown and joined their congregation.

Thus, the church of the open door has become the church of the revolving doors. And the revolving doors go 'round and 'round. Fewer of those who go through them these days do so for reasons of principle or doctrine. They do so for other reasons.

All the way from A to F.

And on to Z.

the chandeliers

Chapter Thirteen

A *chandelier*, according to my dictionary, is a branched, often ornate lighting fixture suspended from the ceiling. It's a French word, I think, meaning "candlestick." I mentioned the other day that I would like a nice one to replace the light in our dining room. It came with the house and, as I said, "didn't do anything for me." The fact is that it does a lot for me; for example, it lights our table at mealtimes. What a miracle electric lights are! God said, "Let there be light"—and there was light. It's almost as easy for me. All I do is flick a switch, and there it is. Alas, we take all these modern conveniences so for granted that, as I said, our dining room light did nothing for me.

My wife reacted in characteristic fashion. Unknown to me, she visited a half dozen lighting emporiums in the city and a week later invited me to inspect several chandeliers that might suit my fancy. Learning their prices instantly increased my appreciation for the light we already had. Even so, I followed my spouse to two different establishments. I was overwhelmed. What an electric bill those people must have! From every available spot on the ceiling hung yet another fixture: lead crystal, beveled glass, tiffany, period classic, gaslight motif, pendants, country coordinates, contemporary, swags. Swags? What are swags? I liked the crystals, but my wife believed they would be too overwhelming in our modest dining room. A tiffany, she thought, might be better.

I wisely agreed and recalled a quote from O. Henry's *Defeat of the City* in which he wrote about somebody's voice that reminded him of the "tinkling of pendant prisms on grand-mother's chandelier." I also remembered my chandelier story: Because the sanctuary's inadequate lighting put half the con-gregation to sleep during his sermons, a pastor proposed the purchase of a rather large chandelier to brighten things up. The matter was discussed at a congregational meeting. Some were in favor. But one solid member, just off the boat, barely man-aging the English language and supposing a chandelier to be some kind of musical instrument, opposed the idea. In his ungrammatical yet eloquent speech against the motion, he pre-sented three grounds for his position. He was against acquiring a chandelier, he said, because probably nobody in that congre-gation of immigrants could spell the word. (This was his con-tribution to the humor of the evening.) His next two reasons were weightier. Probably no one in the church could play one of those things and, in the third place, what they really needed in the sanctuary was a lot more light.

The saleslady showed us the fixtures with a gaslight motif. Instantly I thought of my father. He loved telling about the time when, as a boy in the old country, he and his friend cast the entire congregation into darkness during an evening service. He and his friend were seated by the wall. At their feet was the shutoff valve of the gas line leading to all the lights in the church. My father dared his friend to kick it—just a wee bit—so he did. Then it was my father's turn. And so, two little boys kept daring each other while the sermon droned on and on until, finally, one of them kicked it too far, and all the lights went out.

I used to wonder about that and similar stories. I thought that if I did something like that, I'd probably be killed. Or, worse—excommunicated! Boys in the olden days, I concluded, had a lot more fun.

We went home to think about which tiffany-style chandelier we would buy. We both liked the more expensive of the two, but we had to sleep on the decision. That night I remembered how, when I was a boy in church, I would perform amazing trapeze acts over the heads of the congregation, swinging like Tarzan from chandelier to chandelier to the accompaniment of the sermon. I liked the Detroit Gratiot Avenue Baptist Church, where my friend attended, even better. There you could leap from the balcony to the nearest fixture and then swing to the next, finally landing in the choir loft without once having touched the floor. All in my mind, of course.

At home, falling asleep during the evening news, I dreamt of the talking chandeliers that had hung for centuries in Central Church on Main Street in Mid-America. "Doesn't the new member in the choir look nice?" said one. "I remember her mother," said another. "Yes, and her grandmother," said a third. "But what," asked the first, "has happened to the Joneses? I don't see them anymore. Remember Grandfather Jones? He was a pillar around here." "They're not the only ones missing nowadays," said the center chandelier. "Maybe the sermons aren't what they used to be." Then the smallest chandelier in the balcony piped up: "We went from candles to gas, and then to electricity. How we've changed! But in all those years, the gospel has remained the same. Let's hope the Joneses return like Mary What's-Her-Name. Just think! She was gone awhile, and now she's back and has made profession of faith and is involved in the life of the church. That really turned me on."

Church chandeliers don't speak, of course. But if they did, they would have a lot to say. And I think all would agree that they would rather hang in the house of our God than shine in the tents of wickedness, where people love darkness more than light.

Soon we will have a new chandelier in our dining room.

I think.

Jesus is coming to town

Chapter Fourteen

Even the skeptics were wavering. All the telephones in town had rung simultaneously with the message that Jesus was coming to visit. Special announcements bearing the same information had interrupted the radio and television programs. The following day, mail carriers deposited identical letters in everyone's mailboxes verifying the date.

Widespread doubt followed initial panic. It was a clever hoax! People recalled Orson Welles and his "invasion from Mars" stunt, which had hoodwinked a whole eastern seaboard, if not an entire nation, years ago. But officials from the telephone companies, broadcasting stations, and the post office were at a complete loss. When great cumulus clouds, highlighted by the sun, gathered over the town spelling the announced date, buildings emptied, everyone lifted their eyes, and, as observed, even skeptics began wavered. God might not send postcards from heaven, but this was something else!

The networks quickly scented a story. Reporters, not known for their reticence, arrived to conduct interviews. They asked probing questions. How could a man reappear two thousand years after his death? If he did return, why would he come to a town nobody had ever heard of instead of, say, New York? Some citizens had answers. He came to Bethlehem too, once upon a time, and not, say, Jerusalem.

Ministers preached sermons with Christ's coming in the backs of their minds. They reminded worshipers that, during his lifetime, some towns had spurned him. Some disciples had suggested destruction for such inhospitality. Other sermons pointed out how Jesus had commanded his followers to shake the dust off their feet where they were unwelcome.

A few churches went so far as to plan and organize receptions. Then the whole town was caught up in a fever of anticipation—"crowd psychology," according to experts interviewed on national news networks.

The fundamentalists and the charismatics were not alone in their frenzy. The mainline churches, a little slower emotionally, were a little quicker organizationally. The Council of Churches sought a planned, cooperative approach. They appointed a general chairman, committees, and subcommittees, who developed reports and drew and redrew plans. Gradually, all things took form. They would have a parade. A tree planting. The lighting of an eternal flame. A tour of a local hospital and school. A banquet with a loaves-and-fishes motif, and an evening meeting in Jesus' honor in the Civic Center, tickets being allocated to the churches for distribution on a percentage of membership basis. A cleanup week would precede Christ's visit and, on the day itself, all the theaters would be closed.

Alas, as the great day approached, the plans fell apart. The Roman Catholics insisted on the local bishop for the main address. The Protestants were divided. Some wanted to import Billy Graham for the affair, while others wanted the senior pastor of First Christian on Main Street. The public school superintendent wanted Jesus to visit George Washington High, whereas the Christian and parochial authorities demanded the honor for themselves. They were united only in their opposition to the Washington High idea. After all, Jesus would probably want to offer a prayer, and what would happen if that weren't allowed? Meanwhile, the Civil Liberties Union sent up various warning flares spelling dozens of violations against the principle of the separation of Church and State.

The mayor wondered why he couldn't give the keys of the city to the most famous man who ever lived. The owner of the Triple X Movie House objected to closing his establishment. Scalpers were making a killing off tickets for the evening program at the Civic. The Chief of Police, sensing chaos, was denied additional manpower for budgetary reasons. Merchants were upset by the numerous street hawkers who were selling Jesus T-shirts and other paraphernalia. When everybody was mad at everybody, it happened again. The telephones rang simultaneously with the message that the visit was canceled. Radios and television agreed, and letters from the post office confirmed this. So did cumulus clouds over the town, highlighted by the sun.

No one knows the hour, and that is good. But when he does come, no tickets need be apportioned, for every eye shall see him.

# of body and soul

Chapter Fifteen

A few weeks ago, I saw a movie on television about a brain transplant. Two women were involved. A stroke had claimed the life of one; an auto accident had horribly mangled the body of the other, and she was near death. The stroke victim's body was fine, but her brain was gone. So they did a transplant. They put the good brain of the second woman into the good body of the first.

Can you imagine the results? The women's husbands were terribly confused. One saw his wife's body, alive but inhabited by someone else's brain and spirit. The other saw a stranger who was really his wife. Each woman was now *dead*, yet a living person. I wondered how to apply our definition of *death*—"the separation of the soul from the body." The movie did not deal with any insurance complications. That would have been another kettle of fish.

The whole fanciful concept couldn't possibly happen. Or could it? I went to bed puzzling over the story. I dreamed about it. The next morning my wife and I reviewed it at the breakfast table. Not often does a television drama grab me so completely.

Later that day I had to drive a considerable distance to fulfill a speaking engagement. Still mulling over that movie on television the night before, I turned off the car radio, the better to concentrate. The story wasn't too far-fetched after all. Consider the transplants that have already been successfully accomplished! Unbelievable!

That's when I drifted into my daydream.

I decided to get a new nose. Mine isn't all that bad, but it's a little crooked. Instead of just straightening it, why not get a whole new one? I sent for a catalog on noses. Some big ones were as plain as the you-know-what on your face, and others were smaller and more refined. Some of the ecclesiastical models were pointed a bit too high in the air. There were "nosy" noses for inquisitive persons and the like. I circled one of the aquiline models and went to the institute where they made new people.

The salesperson showed me the price range—all the way from the cheapest (prize-fighter noses) to the class I had selected, which was a bit out of my price range. But I stayed with it. Aquiline was best! Did I want anything else? If so, I might as well have it all taken care of at once. I said I was quite satisfied with the rest of me, except for my hip, which would need a replacement eventually. "Why not now?" the salesperson asked. She also noted that one of my ears stuck out from my head at a rather peculiar angle. I thought of something else too. I had always needed extra padding in the right shoulder of new suits whenever I purchased them. Could that deficiency be corrected? And what about my wrinkles? I could do without them. And—here I hesitated—would it be possible to add to my height? I had secretly always wanted to be about three inches taller.

It was quite a list. Nose. Hip. Ear. Shoulder. Skin. Height. The salesperson said she would give me an estimate. She said I could change now and pay later. I made an appointment.

My new self emerged shortly thereafter. I was quite satisfied, but I noticed that my grandchildren weren't running to me and crawling on my lap as before. My children too seemed somewhat reserved in my presence. My relationship with my wife had altered as well. I had not reckoned with that. I remembered a French short story in which a husband fifty years old suddenly turned twenty-five again. His wife, however, remained at fifty. It ruined their marriage. But, surely, looks are only skin deep! Was my marriage endangered just because I didn't look like me anymore? People no longer listened to my sermons; they talked about my appearance rather than my message.

I began to long for the old me again, warts and all. I went back to the institute where they made new people. Could I have my crooked nose back? I would just as soon keep the new hip, but could they make my one ear stick out from my head at a rather peculiar angle? I showed an old picture of me. Furthermore, I would just as soon have my saggy shoulder like before—and my wrinkles too. Also, I asked whether I could be three inches shorter. All my new suits, which had cost me a bundle, could be altered.

The salesperson said that the institute had never ever had such a request before. Nose. Ear. Shoulder. Skin. Height. But no hip. The salesperson said she would give me an estimate. She said if I paid off the old bill, I could change back and pay later. At this point I shook myself back to reality.

I had arrived at my destination. I checked into a motel. I went into the bathroom and looked in the mirror with a sense of relief. It wasn't much of a face, but it was mine, and I was glad to have it.

Strange how people look for the fountain of youth! If they found it, what would happen to their identities and relationships? The television drama had sparked a long train of thought. Being a preacher, I sought a lesson.

It was not hard to find.

Billions of dollars are spent on physical renewal. Much less on the spiritual kind, even though the latter is far more valuable. People can have new hearts for the asking. They can be turned into new men and women simply by coming to Christ.

They can have their youth renewed like the eagles'. All they need to do is go to him. Ask. Receive.

No estimates.

dreams

Chapter Sixteen

The city had completed its semiannual curb firing, for which all cars had to be off the streets. Curb firing had long ago replaced street cleaners. By this process, all debris was cleanly burned by a centrally controlled electrical system.

I had left my car in the street. The curb firing had damaged my brake chain. (Brake chain?) Using my car anyway, I hurried to my preaching appointment. I barreled down a hill without the restraint of my brake chain. Fortunately, I was able to turn into a street going uphill and, with pounding heart, stop without mishap at the church where I was due. The service was already in progress.

Running down the aisle, I discovered that all in attendance were hearing-impaired Native Americans. As I preached, my words were communicated via smoke signals. I choked on my own sermon and woke up coughing. Too often, I dream of being late for preaching appointments. Quite often, I go back to sleep after waking and continue my dreams. My father could do that too. His dreams were always the same. He was either flying and swooping like a bird over the harbor where he was born, or his trousers were falling down as he was taking the collection in church.

Do dreams mean anything? Sigmund Freud believed a dream was a facade behind which lay a hidden meaning. But Carl Jung claimed dreams had little significance. I'm not so sure. Igor Stravinsky often dreamed about music critics. They were always small rodentlike creatures with padded ears. A. A. Milne said that for every person who dreams of making a million, a hundred dream of being left a million.

Dreams can be very convincing. Some people dream of not being able to sleep and wake up totally exhausted. One man woke up surprised and startled. His wife had slapped him in the face. She had dreamed that he had looked at another woman.

Stephen Foster dreamed of Jeannie with the light brown hair. But Isaac Watts sang of sons forgotten as a dream. Bing Crosby sang too, dreaming of a white Christmas. And what about Martin Luther King? He said, "I have a dream that my four children will one day live in a nation where they will not be judged by the color of their skin but by the content of their character."

Daniel dreamed and wrote it down (Dan. 7:1). Dreams fade easily. Yet they possess a haunting fascination. They mirror events in strange ways. Do they also foreshadow them? Shortly before his assassination, Abraham Lincoln dreamed that he entered a cathedral. At the far side stood a coffin. When he peeked inside it, he saw himself.

Just before midnight, Julius Caesar listened to the inarticulate groans of Calpurnia, who lay beside him. In the morning she told him her dream, in which she had held him bleeding

imagine 69 imagine

and dying. She warned him not to go out that day. He did. It was March 15. The Ides of March! Had Caesar heeded the dream of Calpurnia, his life might have been spared.

Remember the dreams of Jacob, Joseph, Pharaoh, Solomon, Nebuchadnezzar, the Wise Men? Ecclesiastes 5:3 traces many dreams to too much busyness. But God used many others for warnings and predictions. There was Pilate's wife and her message to her husband: "Don't have anything to do with that innocent man, for I have suffered a great deal today in a dream because of him" (Matt. 27:19). I wish I could get into the dreams of all people and say to them, "Have everything to do with that innocent man, Jesus Christ, for he is Savior and Lord of all."

guide for church hoppers

Chapter Seventeen

A weekly column in the local newspaper reports on restaurants and rates them. Recently, another reporter, in my mind, his priorities askew, did the same with churches:

* * * * * * *

We visited ST. ELSEWHERE again. We recommend it for a real adventure. The place has really changed since we visited two years ago. The decor is classier. Stained glass has replaced frosted, and the chandeliers are tiffany-type. Familiar tiny Christmas tree lights outline the steps to the chancel area, and colored lights have replaced the single spotlight focused on the pulpit. Color selections are determined by the sermon subject. The morning we were there, the pulpit was bathed in blue, a cool color to match a sermon on "The Wind," based on Genesis

8:1b ("he sent a wind over the earth"). We noted the water fountain in the narthex with its ever-flowing stream, signifying eternity, while being welcomed by a greeter at the door wearing a
large lapel button flashing the words "God loves you." The
near-perfect acoustics make listening easy. Completely barrier-
free, and easy to find with ample parking and plenty of rest
rooms, this is the ideal church for all those who think they can
only find what they seek elsewhere. We had such a good time
that we have revised our rating of St. Elsewhere from a *B* to an
A-.

* * * * * * *

On the south side of the city, we recommend STRADDLE ON
THE WALL, better known as "The Church with the Handshake."

We cannot recall ever having gone to this church without
having our hand shaken. One of the regular patrons said, "If
you do not 'feel' the welcome, you must be dead." They emphasize the milk of the Word. As a special feature, the Straddle
church calls their nursery room "The Prelude," for obvious
reasons, while they refer to the sanctuary as "The Nursery,"
because we are all children of God. Greeters greet with both
hands as part of a concerted effort at Straddle to emphasize
centrism—a being neither to the right nor left of anything.
Casual dress acceptable. We rate Straddle a straight *B*.

* * * * * * *

North of town a short distance, we recommend THE WILDWOOD.

The Church in the Wildwood (and in a vale) has a beautiful
setting and is a popular spot for vacationers. It's great what you
can do with a barn! We found the bulletins a bit tacky. Our
usher, who told us to call her Sandy, was very friendly. Snag a
window seat if you can. If you're lucky, you might spot some

wildlife in the wildwood. No rest rooms, but the woods are barrier free. Sermons are short. There is much singing. Piano. No organ. We give Wildwood a *C+*.

* * * * * * *

Also on the north side of the city is COMMUNITY.

Always a favorite with us. We expected we would not be disappointed, and we weren't. Take a few moments to drink in the fine atmosphere of the lounge and decide on a wide selection of Sunday morning activities. My wife chose "Sanctuary" and reported the service to be very nice. She especially enjoyed the announcements. I chose the Educational Department in the educational wing, which is much larger than the sanctuary. They hold classes for everything. "Finger Painting" was well attended. They rendered impressions of storms on the Sea of Galilee. Among other offerings, all in the gymnasium, were Spiritual Aerobics, Ecclesiastical Acrobatics, and the one I attended: "Liturgical Dance for Senior Citizens." We rated Community tops last year and see no reason to change our minds. A straight *A*.

* * * * * * *

WESTSIDE PEOPLE'S

If music is your thing, then People's is for you. A few of our musical friends joined us to hear the organ and the choir. The building, a century old, exudes charm, although the dark wood casts a slightly somber air over the place. Not too many present when we attended, but what the crowd lacked in quantity, it made up for in class. The opera-type seats are very comfortable. Certainly a *B+*.

* * * * * * *

ALL SAINTS

The special feature is the brunch, served on the lawn following the short service. Choose from ethnic foods of all nations. The Greek *baklava* and the Dutch *olliebollen* are outstanding. Those who have plans later in the day can attend the early service, but only coffee and cookies are available at that hour. Donations accepted, but not required. No soul goes hungry at All Saints. *A-*.

* * * * * * *

FAITH

We wandered in recently, not knowing what to expect, and found a great emphasis on the meat of the Word. The worshipers sang many songs. Plain bread and wine were served in minimal amounts. We couldn't imagine why the place was so popular. Every seat was filled. We might try it again, but not soon. It's not our cup of tea, and we have too many other exciting places to visit. We rate Faith a *C-*.

* * * * * * *

Brief notices: The Lighthouse—*B* (the pulpit is in the shape of a prow of a ship). The Four Square—*C-* (too much emphasis on foundations). The Old-Fashioned Hour. The Helping Hand. The Circle of Prayer. Ebenezer (hitherto *The Lord Has Helped Us*) are all unrated because we have not visited them.

the sweeper

Chapter Eighteen

My first charge was in Fishagain, the water-wonderland state, in the city of Reborn, made large and famous by Henry Lord I. Fresh from seminary, I was as short on experience as I was long on trepidation. The congregation was kind and encouraging. But it soon discovered the necessity for showing further graces of patience and understanding, for my faults were numerous and my failures not a few. I had some triumphs too. Not many, but what follows is an example of one of my early pastoral "successes."

His first name was Gus, and his last name was Sunergos. Greek by nationality, young and healthy, he was discouraged and suffered greatly from lack of motivation. All this he blurted in the first few minutes of our meeting. Further questioning brought forth more facts, some relevant and others not. I tried to manifest such ministerial deportment as would encourage confidence in me and lead him to share further information. He finally revealed what his trouble was. He hated his job.

He was a sweeper in a broken-down place on West Warring Road. Each day he swept the same floor with the same broom while the minutes dragged and his spirits sagged, for what future did he have? Was there nothing better? Did life have no more to offer? The questions seemed rhetorical, not so much addressed to me as the walls of my small study. With head in hands, he sought no direction. Only commiseration.

Sympathy would not square his shoulders. Platitudes and clichés would never transform this picture of dejection. Why not then, I reasoned, urge upon him a radical course of action? The shock might take his breath away at first. But if he took it seriously, it could bring him new hope and life. So I suggested that he go to the largest and the most famous and successful concern in all of Reborn and apply for a position to the owner and operator himself. Henry Lord! To prevent a quick rejoinder in the negative, I kept talking, elaborating. "Offer not only your services," I said, "but offer yourself. Tell him that you will give your all if he will take you into his organization. It's still a growing company, and, being part of it, you will have a future and all the motivation in the world."

He reacted with incredulity. When he saw I was serious, he indicated that perhaps I had a problem surpassing his, related to my sanity. I answered each argument and objection he raised. As a final rebuttal, he stated that even if he would follow the suggestion, a sweeper, a nobody, would never find entree with the founder and president of the biggest company going. He'd never even get inside the door. I replied that Henry Lord was accessible, that I had talked with him many times, that he was never too busy, and that he never turned anyone away. With that, my visitor took his leave, looking extremely dubious.

During the next few days, Gus continued his intolerable existence as before. He went to Warring Road each morning to sweep and feel sorry for himself. But a seed had been planted. A small inner voice kept prompting him. "Why not try the minister's idea? What do you have to lose?" So his hesitant feet took him to the administration building of the man I had recommended. With his shabby clothes and halting speech, he fully expected rejection. Imagine his surprise when Henry Lord admitted him.

Precisely what went on behind those closed doors between Lord and Gus I cannot tell. But when Gus emerged from that inner office one hour later, he was overcome. Not only had he been offered a job, but a position! Nor was it ordinary; despite his lack of skills, he had been offered nothing less than a partnership in the firm. Incredible!

The next few weeks were dizzying. He was presented with an office across the hall from Henry Lord's. In it he found a collection of the company's books and records (somewhere between sixty and seventy of them) to peruse and study. He was also given an unlimited expense account. If he had need, he had only to go to the top floor where, if he would ask, he would receive. So Gus applied himself to mastering the contents of the company's books. At night he loved to walk on Fishagain Avenue, the main street of Reborn, to see the big Lord Company sign in lights—the sign that was being changed to read "Henry Lord and Gus Sunergos Company." So the young man spent his days while awaiting his special assignment.

He had not even really begun to master those books and records when he received directions as to where to go and what to do. Lord needed him. He could continue his studies even as he worked. So Gus went to the company bank on the top floor, where he had unlimited resources, but where he asked only for enough to cover bus fare.

All this I learned from Gus, who had come to pay me a second visit. He seemed happy and content, a man with a purpose and a joy in living. I hardly recognized him from the old Gus. He was a new man.

"But why did you ask only for bus fare," I asked, "when you could have asked for more?" I knew about that unlimited bank account.

He smiled. "At first you ask for little. It takes time to learn that you can ask for much with confidence."

"But what is your assignment?" I asked, imagining him a director perhaps of some outlying plant, with hundreds working under him. I was eager to know his specific role as a partner in the biggest company going. His answer stunned me.

"I'm a sweeper," he said, "over on West Warring Road." Seeing my surprise, he chuckled and said, "I know. You have questions. And I have few answers. I'm doing what I used to do. And yet—it's all so different now. My senior partner has a special interest, apparently, in that floor at the Warring Plant. So, if it's important to him, it's important to me. Doubt me if you will, but believe me if you can. I'm content."

Gus rose to leave. At the door he turned and said, "I have a good Greek name, but I never knew its meaning. Now that I do, it makes a lot of difference." With that, he stopped out into the street.

Later that evening, I turned to my Greek lexicon, standard equipment in every pastor's study. "*Sunergos*," it said, meaning "laborer together with." The reference was to 1 Corinthians 3:9a. I looked it up. It said, "For we are God's fellow workers . . ."

the sting

Chapter Nineteen

In pursuit of my calling, I had acquired a black thumb. Traveling to a speaking engagement, I had stopped at a restaurant to strengthen the inner man. There I slammed the car door on my thumb. I complained that I would henceforth give more of my time to a safer occupation, such as gardening.

Alas! My resolution did not bring me the safety I sought! Gardening too can be hazardous to one's health. My wife asked me to pick some zinnias from the yard to add to a floral arrangement for the dining room table. One zinnia had a bee on it. Taking exception to my presence, the bee stabbed me on the ear.

The pain was instant and in a class with a crushed thumb. Lesser men would have bellowed fortissimo. Bravely, I only whimpered pianissimo as I ran indoors. My wife removed the stinger, applied an appropriate ointment, and put ice on my afflicted part.

The rest of the day was a total loss. I lay on a wicker couch on the porch, entirely bereft of my zest for life. I wondered whether it might be prudent to cancel my engagement the next day. Two services, with Communion in the morning. Would I be able to put my mind on anything but my wound?

When Sunday came, my ear was swollen and hot. Nevertheless, I was able to give the sacrament and sermon my full attention. During the serving of the bread and wine, however, a crisis arose. Suddenly, as if from nowhere, a bee appeared and began circling the Communion table. Instantly I recognized it as the same bee that had assaulted me and inflicted a nearly mortal wound on the previous day. How did it find me?

It is true, of course, that all bees look alike, and that this one in church could, therefore, be another. There are, I suppose, billions of bees. Even so, a look in its eye marked it unmistakably as the same bee I had met in my garden. It had come to finish me off!

I considered instant flight, but pride and dignity precluded that. I covered the elements of the Communion table hastily and, with a wary eye on my tormentor, remembered something I had read a few days before.

It was an interview in *Centraal Weekblad*, a Dutch church periodical. A small boy had been asked a number of questions about his theological views. Apparently he had thought long and deeply, because his answers were anything but vague.

The boy said that God was 1.4 meters tall and that he weighed thirty kilograms. He sat on a throne. When he tapped with his staff, a servant—an angel—appeared to do his bidding. Of course, the servant never brought him the evening newspaper because God, knowing everything anyway, had no need for one.

The young man was a font of information regarding not only God but also the devil. The latter was just one meter tall but had power to alter his size as circumstances demanded. He could make himself as small as a matchstick or as big as the Euromast, a tall structure that looks down on Rotterdam.

I remembered smiling when I read that article. It gave me good feelings about the childlike faith that our Lord commends. It was refreshing to read a theological interview that required something less than a doctorate to understand.

But as I stood there presiding over the Communion table, it was the satanology of this budding theologian that came to mind. If the devil, I thought, can make himself as small as a matchstick or as tall as the Euromast, and if he could sound like a roaring lion or appear as an angel of light or in sheep's clothing, what would prevent him from materializing in the form of a bee? One thing is sure. He has been pursuing me all my life.

As the service closed, the congregation sang "When peace like a river. . . ." Again, the boy theologian came to mind. Speaking of a spanking he had once received, he had observed that a pain in the heart was more serious than one in the behind. I thought of my ear and agreed. And so, with a sore ear but a healed heart through the love of Jesus, I joined heartily in the singing.

"It is well, it is well"—not with my ear, but with my soul. Praise the Lord!

# of mice and men

Chapter Twenty

The picture turned out well—our granddaughter posing with Mickey Mouse. Disney World is a magic kingdom. So much to see and do! But the high point for our little Chelsea was catching sight of Mickey Mouse and hugging him.

Walter Disney was certainly a genius! Few of us would have been able to build a whole world around a mouse. A mouse is seldom welcome; it is a creature whose appearance in bygone days made ladies leap on chairs yelling "Eek!" Our kindergarten teacher, Miss McCurn, was completely unnerved that day when my friend Stanley let his mouse loose in the classroom. The Bible doesn't rate the mouse very highly either. Along with pigs, mice are unclean (Lev. 11:29; Isa. 66:17).

Even so, mice, who have a way of getting into everything, have also crept into our similes and sayings. "As quiet as a mouse." "When the cat's away, the mice will play." Edna St.

Vincent Millay wrote about life, "which goes on forever, like the gnawing of a mouse."

Walt Disney was not the first to recognize Mr. Mouse's possibilities. Long before Mickey and Minnie was Mother Goose. Children know all about her nursery rhymes, some of which deal with Mickey's ancestors. That crooked man, for example. "He bought a crooked cat, who caught a crooked mouse, and they all lived together in a little crooked house." Pussy Cat traveled all the way to London to see the queen. But what did Pussy Cat do upon arrival? Not much. "I frightened a little mouse under the chair." And what child doesn't know about the mouse that ran up the clock? "When the clock struck one, the mouse ran down. Hickory, dickory, dock."

Aesop's fables are even older than Mother Goose's rhymes. Aesop was a Greek slave who lived about 600 B.C. He wrote animal stories to illustrate human faults and virtues. Although Aesop is more famous than Disney, a visit to Orlando, Florida, suggests that it was the latter's duck (Donald) rather than the former's goose who laid the golden egg. Remember "The Lion and the Mouse"? Heeding the mouse's plea, the king of beasts let the little creature go. Later, when the lion himself was caught in a trap, the mouse gnawed the rope and set him free.

"An act of kindness is a good investment."

Best of all of Aesop's mouse stories is "The Town Mouse and the Country Mouse." When the latter visited the former, he was much more afraid of the dangers of the city than he was attracted by its largess. And so he went home again. "A humble life with peace and quiet is better than a splendid one with danger and risk."

Mighty Mouse! Where others didn't, Walt Disney discerned humanity's preoccupation with humanity's pest and made a mint. Two centuries ago, Robert Burns, the Scottish poet, on turning up a nest with his plough, wrote his famous poem "To a Mouse." And who among us is unfamiliar with C. C. Moore's

" 'Twas the night before Christmas, and all through the house, not a creature was stirring, not even a mouse." My all-time favorite, however, is "Diary of a Church Mouse," written by the late poet laureate of England, John Betjeman. It is the story of a lean, lonely, lowly mouse who lives in the church in a place where the minister never looks; he nibbles on old service books. His bread is sawdust mixed with straw, and his jam is the polish for the floor. Thus he seeks to fill his meager frame.

One service in the year, however, is far greater for him than Easter or Christmas. It is Harvest Festival Sunday (Thanksgiving Day), when worshipers come with corn, loaves of bread, and all manner of food. What a feast for the church mouse! But how troublesome too that other mice, with pagan minds, who have no business there and come on no other Sunday, show up to share his food. Even a rat who denies God's existence turns up and steals a sheaf of wheat. Poor church mouse! Faithful throughout the year, he has to share with "bread Christians" on Harvest Festival Sunday.

No Betjeman, or Burns, or Disney, I tried my own hand at this mouse business some years ago. It was Christian Education Sunday, and the text was taken from the book of Deuteronomy (6:4-9). This familiar passage instructs parents to teach their children with all diligence—"when you sit at home and when you walk along the road, when you lie down and when you get up. Tie them as symbols on your hands and bind them on your foreheads. Write them on the doorframes of your houses and on your gates." Christian education, it seems, must be all-consuming and all-pervading. It is no part-time thing.

In casting about for an illustration, I settled on the lowly mouse. "Consider Mr. Mouse," I said, "and his total concentration in teaching mousemanship to his children. It is no part-time thing. He doesn't care to have any of his offspring turn into something else. He doesn't teach birdmanship, however interesting. He doesn't teach ratmanship. When he sits in his house, when he walks along the road, when he lies down and gets up, his whole being is concentrated, and without interruption, on teaching mousemanship. He ties it as symbols on his hands, binds it on his forehead, and he writes *mousemanship* in great big letters on the doorframes of his house and on his gates."

I forget the punch line. But the application is not easy to miss. Teaching mousemanship is a full-time task. So is Christian education; it involves home, church, and school.

We bought Chelsea one of those mouse caps at Disney World. I put it on. It reminded me of those Mouseketeers on ancient television programs. It also reminded me of my old sermon on mousemanship.

Not the greatest in the world. But the illustration wasn't all that bad.

family troubles

Chapter Twenty-One

Reading between the lines of the Old Testament the other day, I ran across an interesting set of letters printed in the *Canaan Gazette* and answered by the Counselor, the ancient counterpart of Ann Landers and Abigail VanBuren of syndicated fame.

Dear Counselor:
I have twelve sons, the youngest two of whom are by my favorite wife. One of them is still a baby; the other, Joseph, is a real comfort. He is thoughtful and obedient. The problem is that the ten older boys resent him. If they merely taunted and teased him, I wouldn't worry so much, because I guess some of this is normal. But they actually hate him. I can see it in their eyes.

What can I do? I have rewarded Joseph because he deserves it. The other day I gave him a nice coat. The others didn't prove their worth, so they didn't get one. I thought it would be an incentive to them to become better boys. I do like Joseph best; so would you, I think. Sometimes I reprimand him—like the time he had a silly dream in which we all bowed down to him. Privately, though, I think that something like that could happen. At least, I'm sure he will go farther in life than the others. But what can I do about this family situation? It's really got me down. I'd like some peace and quiet when I read the paper. Shall I tell the ten older ones to move out? Or shall I side with them? What can I do for some peace and quiet around here?

"Cheated by the Dozen"

Dear "Cheated": See below.

Dear Counselor:

I have a problem. My baby brother is okay, but ten bigger ones have it in for me. They are not nice. They should use better language and be more respectful of our dad. I try to be obedient, so my father likes me better than them. The other day he bought a nice jacket for me but not the others. They are jealous and call me "sissy" and other names.

Don't think I'm crazy, but I really believe that someday my brothers will look up to me. I had some dreams that I think were from God, in which not only my brothers but even the sun, moon, and stars bowed down to me. I told my brothers about these dreams, but this only made them angrier than ever. Why? Do you think the fact that they are my half-brothers has anything to do with it? I would really like to be friends with them. What did I do wrong?

"Daddy's Boy"

Dear "Daddy's": See above and below.

Dear Counselor:

We are ten brothers with one common headache. Baby brother Ben is okay, but little brother Joseph is driving us all out of our gourd. We think he needs a headshrinker, but our poor blind father, who otherwise can see pretty good, seems to think that, compared to Joey-boy, we are all a bunch of hoods. The little brat gets fed the best of everything, while we just get fed up. Dad bought him a sport coat the other day, which he must have picked up out of that pot they say is at the end of the rainbow. It's not a jacket; it's a color tour, and it's got us drooling real good. How come we never got one? And why does little Lord Fauntleroy have to wear his rag in front of us all the time like it was red and we were bulls?

Our little nightmare has dreams too. The other day he bragged about one in which our sheaves bowed to his sheaves. In another, he said the sun and stars bowed down to him, which didn't even happen to ancestor Abraham. Frankly, we are getting real sick of this pill. Nor do we like this favorite-son act of our father. You'd think Dad would know it hurts—he told us that when he was a kid, he also had a brother who got the preferential bit.

Help! Before we do something to you-know-who.

"Ten Brothers Grimm"

Dear "Ten": See above.

* * * * * * *

In my opinion, Counselor was wise to refer all parties to each other's points of view. Many of our family clashes might be avoided if everyone would take the time to see the issues from the other's side. It helps, sometimes, to stand in each other's shoes.

Inasmuch as this family situation came to its crisis around a piece of wearing apparel, it is too bad that Counselor did not have available to him Colossians 3:12-14, which also deals with the elect's wardrobe. The passage is, however, available to us and useful in the maintenance of good relationships inside and outside the family.

Therefore, as God's chosen people, holy and dearly loved, clothe yourselves with compassion, kindness, humility, gentleness and patience. Bear with each other and forgive whatever grievances you may have against one another. Forgive as the Lord forgave you. And over all these virtues put on love, which binds them all together in perfect unity.

chain reaction

Chapter Twenty-Two

I

Mr. Tycoon was ready to explode. What had gone wrong? Who dropped the ball? The deal would have brought him national attention. He had been promised that it was in the bag, but now, because of some incompetent jerk in his organization, the whole business had soured. Mr. Tycoon was so mad he chewed out Mr. Division Manager, who happened to call on the phone about a trifling detail. Mr. Division Manager, who had no connection with the department in which things had gone wrong, bore the brunt of Mr. Tycoon's all-consuming ire.

II

Mr. Division Manager drove home, licking his wounds. The heavy rush-hour traffic did not improve his mood. Mr. Tycoon could jump in the lake.

Mr. Division Manager scolded himself for taking all that guff lying down. He should have gone upstairs and punched His Highness in the nose! That's exactly what he would have done—except that it would have been economic suicide. Groveling was the price he had to pay. With two in college and two at home, he had mouths to feed.

Mr. Division Manager parked the car in the garage and stomped into the house. His wife met him with the news that dinner would be late. She had gone shopping and had run out of gas. Mr. Division Manager took his resentment against his boss out on his wife. "You're always running out of something!" he said. He slammed a door.

III

Mrs. Division Manager felt hurt. Here she was, slaving for her husband, and did he appreciate it? The more she thought about it, the more angry she became. Just then her nine-year-old daughter wandered in and asked for help. She couldn't find her piano lesson book. "Shut up and don't bother me," answered Mrs. Division Manager.

IV

Miss Nine-Year-Old was so mad at her mother that she went outside and kicked the dog. Spot whimpered. Two minutes later, Spot came back and nuzzled his young mistress and licked her hand.

III

Miss Nine-Year-Old was sorry she had kicked Spot. She felt even worse when her dog returned her unkindness with love. She was smarting because her mother had bitten her head off. But if Spot had been so nice to her after she had been so mean to him, maybe she ought to learn a lesson from her pet and go into the house and be nice to her mother. She found her mother in the kitchen and took her hand. "I love you, Mom," she said.

II

Mrs. Division Manager was deeply moved. She had been short with her daughter, but her daughter had not repaid her in kind. She had been thinking of ways to get even with her husband. But, of course, that was not Christian. And her daughter had to be the one to remind her not to return evil for evil! She prepared a cup of Cafe Vienna, her husband's favorite hot drink, and brought it to him. "I'm sorry," she said. "You told me to gas up, and I forgot. My fault." She handed him the cup. "A peace offering," she said. She smiled and gave him a kiss.

I

Mr. Division Manager was back in the office the next day. He was thinking about a verse in Proverbs. His wife's loving response to his gruff behavior had reminded him of Solomon's words: "A gentle answer turns away wrath, but a harsh word stirs up anger" (Prov. 15:1). He decided to go upstairs. Maybe he would run into Mr. Tycoon. He would wish Mr. Tycoon a good day. After all, if his wife could practice charity at home, he could surely try to practice it at work. Mr. Tycoon came around the corner. Mr. Division Manager smiled at him and said, "Good morning. It's a beautiful day." Mr. Tycoon looked surprised. Life was tough, but somehow Mr. Division Manager, whom he had unjustly mistreated only yesterday, just made his day. He smiled.

If God can use a dog to turn things around, he can surely use you to do the same.

spare tire

Chapter Twenty-Three

Is something wrong with me? I was sitting on a quiet stretch of road. Quite literally. Not in the car, but right down on the pavement with my feet out in front of me. It was six-thirty in the morning, and I was talking to a tire.

A young man drove by. He stopped, reversed, and stuck his head out of the window. Did I need help? I declined his kind offer and thanked him. What a fine chap! He looked like a Calvin College student. The salt of the earth! A Christian! A good Samaritan! His parents could be proud of him. But had he seen me talking to my tire? He had a question in his eyes as he shifted gears and left—a little too fast, I thought.

I had come home late the night before from a church council meeting. Pulling into the garage, I was worried to find our other car, a rusted-out yellow Plymouth station wagon, missing. I recalled that I had told it that very morning, in a private con-

versation on the way to the gas station, that we would be replacing it soon with a new model. I had patted it on its steering
wheel as I imparted the sobering news. Was that why it was
missing? Had it gone off somewhere in a huff? All by itself?
But, of course, that was ridiculous. Automobiles are inanimate
objects. They cannot hear. They cannot speak. But where, then,
could my wife have gone with it at such a late hour? Surely
nobody would steal it!

Inside the house, my wife called down from the upstairs bed-
room. "Had a blowout. Had to walk all the way home. The car
is on the Beltline. On the ramp by Calvin College." That was
not what I needed to hear. Tomorrow would be an unusually
busy day. The only thing to do was to get there early—at dawn.

It dawned on me the next morning that I had not changed a
tire in years. I remembered my first car, an ancient Model-T
Ford that I had bought, with a friend, for five dollars. We drove
it fifty miles to a campsite, taking turns fixing twenty-one flats.
It took all day. As I reminisced, I looked forward to my chal-
lenge. Would there be enough air in the spare?

As I removed the tire from its housing, I noted its prime condition: a radial whose rubber had never yet hit the road. I wondered how I would like to be a tire that was never used. That
would be like a ball player spending the whole season on the
bench. I wondered what my spare tire thought, in its dark hole
all these years, listening to its four whirling, singing, spinning
brothers gleefully peeling off thousands of highway miles. How
terrible, I thought, not to be doing what you were made for. It
was at this point that I began talking to my tire. "Now it's your
turn," I said. "It must have been hard for you never touching
the road all this time while listening, in the dark, to your peers
underneath. Of course, you'll not look as new now, but so
what—it's better to be useful." Then I looked up into that college student's face and wondered, as he sped off, "Is something

wrong with me? Has anyone else in the world ever held a conversation with a tire?"

Come to think of it, I do the same with stones. I always kick them when I encounter them on the sidewalk, even though my wife says it's bad for my shoes. I always figure that stones appreciate a change of scenery. "There," I say, toeing one into the bushes, "you're probably tired of the sidewalk; you'll like it better in the shade." But is this abnormal too? I remember that Clarence, my boyhood friend, once talked to a hammer. We were building a birdhouse together when he hit his thumb with it so hard that he cried. He took that hammer and hurled it against the side of the garage. Then he grabbed a saw and sawed off its handle. "You'll never hit anybody's thumb again," he said. "Serves him right," I added approvingly. But do others, too, talk to things?

People talk to babies, often unintelligibly. They say "goo goo" and things like that, even to one-day-olds. It's probably just as normal to talk sense to a tire as nonsense to an infant. People also talk to plants. A woman in a television ad does it all the time. They say this is good for them. Lord Tennyson talked to a "flower in the crannied wall." He said, "I pluck you out of the crannies." Even so, I don't remember my English literature teacher speculating that Tennyson was strange for doing this. As a minister, I can say that flowers and tires probably listen a lot better than some congregations I have addressed.

When I didn't listen, my father would sometimes say in exasperation, "I might as well talk to the wall." But, today, we know that walls have ears. Aside from hidden microphones, sound waves leave impressions on surfaces. All we need, say scientists, is the invention of a machine that will play our conversations back to us—right off the wall! What a thought!

Personification is attribution of personal nature or character to inanimate objects. And so some people cry when they trade in their old trusty cars for newer ones. They even talk to them.

Today, cars talk to us too. The new one I tried last week didn't
startle me at all when it said quietly, "Fasten your seat belt,
please." Yesterday a computer called me on the phone, and I
talked to it. Some day people will talk to mountains. They
already have. Did you ever read Luke 23:30? "Then they will
begin to say to the mountains, 'fall on us' and to the hills, 'cover
us.'"

But back to my spare tire—not on me, but on my car. Maybe
it didn't hear me. But maybe someone else will, as I para-
phrase: Be of service to God and neighbor. You will not look as
nice or new, perhaps, but "so what—it's better to be useful."
That's why God made us.

God doesn't want any of us to be spare tires.

sef

Chapter Twenty-Four

His name was Josef, but they called him "Sef" for short. An accident at birth had left him mentally impaired and an orphan besides. Had he lived in more modern times, and in the city, he might have benefited from such special attention and education and schools as exist today for the handicapped. But he was born a hundred years ago. And he lived in a small Austrian village, nestled in a narrow mountain valley. Its main street was guarded by shops on either side, the church at the end of it, from which the street had received its name: *KircheStrasse*. Sef had been baptized in that church, and now he lay in its yard at the edge beneath a stone that simply read, "Here rests in Christ," and then, no date of birth or death or even a family name, just "Sef."

In all his days, Sef never saw the other side of the mountain. The village was his whole world. It was a good world whose peaceful familiarity enfolded him. Villages, unlike impersonal cities, are places where the town drunk is talked about in private and prayed over in public, but always treated with kindness. So too the village idiot. And though Sef was far from either condition, he required a certain amount of care and love and received it from all of his fellow townspeople.

When Sef was old enough to work, the village council decided that he must be given something to do. Living on handouts was not good for his self-respect. They appointed him captain of the street. It was his responsibility to sweep Kirche-Strasse every morning and evening. Sef received a cart, broom, and shovel, and for nearly a half century, KircheStrasse was the cleanest street in all the province.

Every Monday morning, rain or shine, Sef was on the job. By 7:00 A.M. the street was always swept. Then the children would come hopping and skipping their way to school. Mrs. Goetz would hold up her baby to the window for Sef to wave to. She started a tradition; thereafter, all babies were held up to the window for him to wave to—even toward the end when he couldn't see well anymore and missed pieces of paper in the street. On Saturday evenings he worked later than usual because the oompah band always played in front of the hotel. Afterward, he always put his cart and broom and shovel away till Monday mornings, because Sunday was the Lord's Day when he went to the church. He didn't always understand the minister. But he understood when the sermon taught that Jesus wants us all to be faithful in our work.

Sef was supposed to sweep the KircheStrasse only mornings and evenings, but he became so attached to his job that he took to cleaning it every noon as well. He also began helping old ladies with canes, shopkeepers with window washing, and strangers who needed directions. Sef always welcomed window shoppers and strollers to enjoy "his street," as he called it.

The greatest day in his life was when Hans Weisenheimer came to visit. Hans had been baptized the same day as Sef, in the same church. But Hans had gone to the other side of the mountain and become rich and famous. The village council had invited Hans back so that they could honor him. Right where the oompah band usually played, they had a ceremony with speeches and flags. Afterward, everybody celebrated with beer and schnapps. Sef had cleaned the street that morning with extra care and afterward had worked till midnight clearing the debris. At the height of the reception for Hans, the village mayor, with the unanimous support of the council, had declared that the name *KircheStrasse* was now forever changed to *WeisenheimerStrasse*.

The saddest day in Sef's life was even busier. If the whole town had come out to honor Hans, the whole province, in procession, gathered soon after for his funeral. They buried him in the churchyard in a place of honor. The immense stone was beautifully inscribed. The village council gave Sef the additional responsibility of watering the flowers on Hans's grave each day. Sef was proud to do it. And he continued, Mondays through Saturdays, three times a day, to sweep what used to be *KircheStrasse* and was now changed to *WeisenheimerStrasse*.

One day they found Sef beside his cart. He was dead. A small procession followed his coffin to the churchyard. On the way, old Mrs. Goetz's son dropped his cigar butt.

The next morning it was still there.

It all happened a few years ago. Today, the town is bigger and always filled with tourists. A whole sanitation crew now keeps the city, including *WeisenheimerStrasse,* clean. But the angels in heaven have a different name for it. They still call it "Sef's Boulevard."

christmas tree

Chapter Twenty-Five

Last year the Chicago Museum of Science and Industry displayed a marvelous exhibit of Christmas trees of all nations. They were tall and beautiful. The Polish tree held stars, angels, and peacocks. From the Swedish tree dangled painted wooden ornaments. In Denmark, Christmas trees are covered with mobiles of bells, stars, snowflakes, hearts, and tiny Danish flags. Japanese Christians adorn their trees with tiny fans and paper lanterns. Straw birdcages and geometric shapes decorate Lithuanian trees. The Chicago Museum of Science and Industry is simply wondrous for adults and children alike, worth miles of travel to see. Even so, nothing it contained fascinated me more last December than its display of trees. After inspecting them all, I started over and looked a second time. "You shall be witnesses for me to the uttermost parts of the earth," said Jesus. And here was the evidence of the gospel's reach: Christmas trees of all the nations!

Does this explain my fascination with last year's Chicago show? Perhaps, but I turn to a deeper explanation. I trace my love for the Christmas tree to childhood days when those at our house considered them a sin. Accordingly, we had none. Our neighbors, few of whom went to church, all had Christmas trees I secretly admired. Stanley's mother even put angels and the Christ Child in the branches of their tree. I disapproved outwardly. I even told Stanley that he and his parents were pagans. Not knowing what pagans were, he hit me in the mouth anyway. And I hit him back. I deserved it. I condemned Stanley, but I wanted a tree. I was the hypocrite.

I would not exchange my Christian upbringing. I thank the Lord for my godly parents. Still, in those days, good Christian Reformed people may have been a little too much on the somber side. The Dominie was correct when he told us that Christmas trees sprang from the Druid priests' practice of worshiping the oak. The Egyptians, Romans, and Germans also observed winter tree ceremonies. In spite of this, it was great fun each year to attend the Lutheran Christmas program. In the sanctuary for all to see stood a gaily lighted tree so tall that it reached the ceiling. "O Tannenbaum, O Tannenbaum." By contrast, our own church looked drab and dull.

I was delighted when father finally relented, and we had a tree of our own. He struggled with his conscience mightily, and some remonstrated with him. But I think he did the right thing. And so, this year we shall have one again, even if, to save some dollars and our forests, it will be the artificial one we bought a few years back. I enjoy it. Rather than detracting from, it adds to my Christmas glow as I meditate on the greatest gift of all.

For this reason I write about the Christmas tree. Christian parents miss a great opportunity when they fail to connect Christmas trimmings and trappings with the Bethlehem event.

Tell the children of the joy their own birth occasioned and the ensuing announcements, presents, and visitors. How much more, then, should we celebrate the birth of our Lord! Every way we can! With special services, and music, and colors, and lights—and trees. You can even tell them stories about the Christmas tree. Make them up. If Hans Christian Andersen and Christopher Morley could, so can you. Use your imagination. Here are two of mine.

* * * * * *

Once upon a time there was a little evergreen. It grew to a perfect height—not too small and not too tall. It stood on the side of a hill. When winter came, snow rested on its shoulders and looked so beautiful that it caught the eye of a little girl. "That's the tree I want," she said to her parents and brother. And so they cut it down and took it home with them.

The tree was flattered to be chosen and felt even more honored to be taken into the little girl's home. The family placed it not in the closet or basement, but by the window in the living room. Then they decorated the tree with their prettiest things—baubles and bells and lights and candy canes. They piled presents around the tree. Everybody said the tree gave the house a nice smell, and visitors all exclaimed about the beautiful, beautiful tree. On Christmas Day, they all gathered around it and opened their presents. It was all so wonderful! The tree thought it would burst! But the next morning, the day after Christmas, the family stripped the tree of all the baubles and bells and angels and lights and candy canes, dragged it outside, and dumped it by the curb.

Too bad, isn't it, that so many, when Christmas is over, treat the Savior the very same way.

* * * * * *

Bill and June lived all alone, way up north, along the shores of Georgian Bay. It was December. Christmas was coming, and not a soul was around. "It doesn't seem like Christmas," said Bill, "with no one to celebrate." "I'm here," said June, smiling, and added, "why don't we celebrate Christmas by decorating the living room and dressing up the big evergreen outside. We have a lot of Christmas tree lights and plenty of extension cords. Imagine how nice it will look!"

"But no one will see it," Bill said. He remembered when they lived in the city and people would drive around to see each other's Christmas decorations. Just the same, they put the lights on the tree. Lit up, it looked so nice! When they went to bed, they left on the lights. Just like the beautiful flower in the forest that only God sees, so Bill and June's tree beautified the solitary night. But in the middle of it, a loud noise wakened them. Through the window they saw a freighter flashing all its lights and blowing its whistle. The captain had seen their Christmas tree and called all hands on deck. All the men cheered at the sight, because it reminded them of home. Indeed, one sailor, who had run away and was feeling lonely and sad, decided, on seeing the lighted tree, to return home as soon as he could.

If a Christmas tree can do that, how much more ought we do to brighten the corners where we are!

push! push!

Chapter Twenty-Six

Fill your mouth with air. Let your cheeks balloon. Imagine that your head is a tire with too much air pressure inside. Quickly unseal your lips. As the air rushes out, say the word *push.*

Try it again. At the point of release, your lips should be in the proper position for the letter *p* of the word *push.* Practice. Give the letter *p* a slightly explosive quality. Got it? Push! Push!

Many years ago I saw a television program about a tycoon. He was overweight. He had jowls, folds of flesh hanging from his jaw. He was berating the salesmen who were his employees, giving one of his frequent lectures. He was telling them to "Push! Push!" "You don't get anywhere in this world just contemplating your navel," he said. "The early bird gets the worm. 'Go to the ant, you sluggard,' says the Bible"—and all that sort of thing. He got so worked up by his own lecture that beads of perspiration sprang forth upon his brow. His sentences got shorter, along with his breath, till finally he summed it all up with just one word: *push.* "Push! Push! Push!" As his enormous cheeks expanded and deflated each time he said the word and his jowls fluttered like aspen leaves and his sweaty lips flapped in his own exhaling breeze, the camera zeroed in on the lower part of his face while the sound technician switched on the echo chamber, prolonging each "Push!" to a haunting vibration.

("The business of America is business."—Calvin Coolidge)

One of the salesmen of Mr. "Push! Push!" was going through a hard time. His father was dying of cancer, and his wife was experiencing a difficult pregnancy. No wonder he was preoccupied! Concentrating on his work was hard. He had lost an account, and his sales were down. The boss noticed. He summoned him to that inner sanctum that was his office. Mr. "Push! Push!" took the big cigar out of his mouth. He couldn't say "Push! Push!" very well with his cigar in it. He paced. He pumped up his employee. "Go get 'em!" he said. "Up and at 'em!" he added. "Push! Push! Push!"

Calidus has traded about thirty years in the greatest city in the kingdom. Every hour of the day is with him an hour of business, and though he eats and drinks very heartily, yet every meal seems to be in a hurry, and he would say grace if he had time. . . . He does business all the time that he is rising, and has settled several matters before he can get to his counting room. His prayers are a short ejaculation or two, which he never misses . . . because he always has something or other at sea. . . . He is now so rich he would leave off his business, and amuse his old age . . . but he is afraid he would grow melancholy if he was to quit his business. . . . If thoughts of religion happen at any time to steal into his head, Calidus contents himself with thinking that he has never been a friend to heretics and infidels, that he has often been civil to ministers of his parish, and very often given something to the charity schools.

—William Law (1686-1761), from
A Serious Call to a Devout and Holy Life

On the telephone Mr. "Push! Push!" was fuming to his wife about their sixteen-year-old. "When is that kid gonna learn?" he asked. "Sitting on your bottom never gets you to the top." That evening he would have a talk with his teenager—something he seldom had time for. He would give his favorite lecture on "Push! Push! Push!"

"Heart" is still the number one killer. In some eastern cultures a storekeeper closes shop at midmorning, noon, or midafternoon—whenever he has made the daily quota which he needs to live. In our western culture, the shopkeeper remains open all the day. In our western culture, we have two types. Type B might well fit in with the more relaxed eastern tradition. Type A is aggressive, driven, and makes the world go around. Most heart attack victims are Type A.

—from a lecture by Agnippe, 1984

Mr. "Push! Push!" drove home, accompanied by a briefcase stuffed with work to attack after dinner. He had to "Push! Push!" He was sitting on top of the heap because he practiced what he preached. To stay on top he had to push some more. His foot got the message too and pushed too hard on the accelerator as he passed the recreation center. He had an accident. He was killed. He would push no more.

On the recreation field, a hundred feet away, little boys in baseball uniforms were sobbing their hearts out. They were inconsolable. They had just lost the big game. They would not be Little League champions. All season their coach had told them that they had to win at all costs. Winning was more important than fun. More important than anything. Winning was American. "O Say! Can You See?" and all that stuff. As the wail of an ambulance approached the accident victim on the corner, the coach told his weeping players that they would have to push harder next year.

I don't really remember that television program of years ago. Only the "Push! Push!" part. The story you just read was made up to remind a lot of us to "Take Time to Be Holy." Switch on the echo chamber. Holy . . . holy . . . take time.

yummie

Chapter Twenty-Seven

Sweetie Strident is a highly paid television personality. She has talent. She also lives by the firm belief that the meek shall not inherit the earth. It is said that, on camera, Sweetie renders her subjects so transparent that no secrets are hidden from the nation's eyes. No wonder that the male half of the country tuned in when she held an "in-depth" sixty minutes of conversation with Yummie Atlas.

Yummie Atlas is a highly paid movie star. He has a little talent. He lives by the firm belief that the poor in spirit shall not inherit the kingdom of earth. He specializes in showing off rows of gleaming teeth and flexing his enormous muscles. He does this better than most. He is also an expert at long looks and heavy breathing. It is said that, on camera, Yummie's behavior, which leaves virtually nothing hidden or sacred, renders his female audiences helpless. No wonder that the other half of the nation also tuned in recently when he engaged in an "in-depth" sixty minutes of leering at Sweetie Strident, who was holding an "in-depth" sixty minutes of conversation with him.

By prime time of the appointed evening, most Americans had settled into their television chairs. Sweetie and Yummie materialized with an omnipresence that extended from border to border, and from sea to sea and beyond. The sight gladdened the hearts of all. Strident moved across the Atlas living room in a skimpy dress, while Yummie relaxed in a shirt that accentuated his muscles. They smiled at each other and at America before fading away and being replaced by a huge armpit.

It was a commercial, praising the superior features of Armamint, an underarm deodorant. Without this product, Sweetie and Yummie would never have met success. Indeed, the only place in the whole wide world where anyone could be completely safe these days was under the arm—"armed" with Armamint. Without Armamint ye have not put on the whole armor.

Strident and Atlas returned to the screen. They were strolling through Yummie's grounds, home of seven swimming pools. He had a thing about swimming pools. He had been "discovered" by the side of one back in those days when he had lived in Brooklyn, in abject poverty. Though Sweetie was supposed to be doing the interviewing, she seemed, instead, to be doing all the talking. Finally she interrupted herself long enough to ask a question, her eyes wide, innocent, and fluttery. "But, Yummie, seven swimming pools? Seven!" Yummie opened his yummie mouth. When he was a lifeguard living in abject poverty in Brooklyn, he vowed he would one day be rich and own seven swimming pools. He flexed his muscles and gave the cameras a long look that indicated that seven was unquestionably a logical number of pools to possess.

Another commercial. Millions of men and women and little children, and older ones too, were introduced to Contour

Bras—for all moods and for all occasions. And guess what, America! The familiar theme song for Contour Bras was being incorporated into two movements of a symphony Andre Previnga was writing for the Philadelphia. Yippie!

Sweetie and Yummie swam into focus again, though neither was in any of the pools. Instead, they were comfy and cozy in the billiard room. Yummie never played billiards. But back in the Brooklyn abject poverty days, he had vowed a billiard room would be thrown in along with all those pools. And, surely, a man must always be true to his vows! Yummie could be so funny.

Sweetie laughed softly. Then she grew strident again. Speaking of vows, how come he quit living with Ida? And what about his new roommate—what's her name? Sweetie touched a bulging biceps muscle on Yummie's right upper arm. He grew serious.

Ida was the best. When God made her, he threw the mold away. Anybody who got funny with Ida would have to reckon with him. As for Linda, his new roommate, that was different.

"Are you going to marry her?"

He was spiritually married to her already. What was marriage? A piece of paper and a wedding, or a real feeling, like you wanted to act and be in a movie with Linda forever?

"What do you do when diarrhea comes to visit?" Just another commercial, although, following Ida and Linda, it sounded like another name. Whoever said that television shows were superficial? This advertisement clearly dealt with the inner person. So remember, how do you spell *relief*? R.E.L.I.E.F.!

Sweetie was on camera again, close up. You could tell that she was a year older than five years ago. She looked serious. You could tell she was going to lay something heavy on Yummie.

"When did you—if you know what I mean—become a man?"

"College."

"That late? Thank you for being honest. Most would have said high school, even if it wasn't true. But another question. On a scale of one to ten, where would you rate yourself as to looks?"

Yummie thought awhile. The question required some concentration. Finally, he answered.

"Ten."

"Yummie Atlas, I want to thank you for this look into your life. America thanks you too. Please, don't change. We like you as you are, and we look forward to seeing you in your next production. Good night, America."

The camera zoomed in on a Sweetie tooth, followed, quite appropriately, by a commercial for mouthwash.

A nation is known by its heroes.

a modern yankee in solomon's court

Chapter Twenty-Eight

Dear King, Your Honor, you sure got a nice country. I mean it's got everything. I've been rattling around it for weeks, and I've seen it all from Gilead to Dan. I've looked at Naphtali, the Land of Ephraim and Manasseh, and all the Land of Judah to the sea. I've seen the south, and the Plain of the valley of Jericho, the city of palm trees, all the way to Zoar. I've seen it all, better than Moses saw it from Mount Nebo and the top of Pisgah.

Like I said, you sure got yourself a great little country here. It kind of reminds me of my own. Our forefathers were pioneers just like yours. In both cases, they went for the land of milk and honey. Sure, it wasn't easy. But it all added up to a lot of money for both of us.

That's what I want to talk to you about, O King, Your Honor. Money. You got a reputation for brains. I heard that story about those two babies. You're a wise guy, and I don't mean any dis-respect. You sure built the country a real cathedral, even though I would have made it more functional. The services ought to be revved up some too, but then, I don't know much about that. Anyway, I've got more to say about this later.

Right now, though, I want to say something about business. I think that right here, you're as good as they come. The stock quotations went up again last week. Your trade relations with those other countries is a real balance. You got this import-export thing right down to a science. The thing is though, O King, Your Honor, that you've barely scratched the surface. Everywhere I look I see opportunities with dollar signs, even though I'm not half as smart as you.

Take all those beauty spots in your country, plus all the historical sites, and you got yourself a gold mine. I wish I could show you our Niagara Falls. We surrounded it with souvenir shops, motels, hamburger joints, and hot spots. We know how to milk those waters a hundred different ways—making money for everybody. I tell you, O King, Your Honor, there's all kinds of ways to make a buck, and not just out of nature. I'd like to show you how we've capitalized on some of our Civil War battle locations. We could do the same thing with your old city of Jericho if you'd sell it to us. We'd move it, brick by brick, put it somewhere, and make it a tourist attraction at twenty bucks a head. But you can do it, right where it is. You people tend to make these things into shrines. You put up altars. But where's the money in that?

You know what I'd do with your Sea of Galilee? I'd make it the site for an annual international sailing regatta. The winner gets to kiss your toe. It'd be the sporting event of the year. And it would pull in a lot more shekels than all your Galilean fish put together and sold in the marketplace.

Speaking of the Sea of Galilee, know what you can do with your Jordan River? Give me the word and I'll see to it that you get some yearly hydroplane races there. Sure, it would pollute the water some, but all that clean aqua is still no money in the bank. I could get you hundreds of powerboats and crew members. And I'll guarantee you thousands of spectators. Let the fishermen howl. They don't own that river. You do.

Of course, you could argue that all those spectators might, like, spoil the landscape with their litter. Some people in our country are always squawking about nature. But I could take care of that. I'd arrange to have about two thousand motor-cyclists patrol the riverbanks. They could keep order among the spectators, pick up the beer cans, and rescue whatever fishermen were stupid enough to get in the way of those eighty-mile-an-hour hydroplanes. I figure that two events a year like this could add up to millions for the economy.

Now don't you worry, O King, Your Honor, if you don't get it when I talk about hydroplanes, motorcycles, and the rest. I got it covered. Leave all these things to me.

What you got to do for your part, O King, Your Honor, is to deemphasize that cathedral you built, which I mentioned earlier. Also you got to deemphasize the Sabbath, because if you don't, people won't have weekends. And without weekends, the regattas on the Galilee and the races on the Jordan, plus all the other ideas I got, are dead.

If you'll just think about the revenue, I'm sure you'll do something about that Sabbath and the cathedral. Just like we did. Because, like everybody knows, O King, you're a smart king, Your Honor.

bon appetit

Chapter Twenty-Nine

Why did they have to sing so many verses! He was tired out with two more to go. He glanced down and sucked in his stomach. All the verses finished, he sat down, after which the minister announced his text: "Let your moderation be known unto all men." He said it was from Philippians and from the King James. His wife poked him discreetly. She couldn't remember. Had she turned the oven on? How annoying! The last time she couldn't remember, it had been off, and she had microwaved the meat. That was no way to treat an expensive roast. He was of the old school. Slow simmer! That was the only way to bring the beef to full flavor. He gave his wife his long-suffering look as if to say, "Too late to check now." The best thing to hope for was a short sermon followed by a quick homeward dash to the oven—and the roast.

He looked at the woman in the pew ahead. He and his wife were due at her house immediately after the evening service for Bible study. He was less interested in these monthly affairs since they had limited refreshments to coffee and cookies. What a shame. He had received much more from the sessions when they had been accompanied by the culinary competition of the hosts.

No harm done though. He was now president of the church's newest organization, the "Food from Bible Lands" Club. He remembered some of last year's meetings. At each one they had studied a different Old Testament feast. What a way to learn the Bible! With knife and fork they had studied the feasts of Dedication, Passover, Purim, Tabernacles, and Trumpets. He had liked the last one best. They had served Duckling Biga-rade, Lobster Savannah, and Steak Lafayette. As Harry said, "If they didn't serve those dishes at the Feast of the Trumpets, they sure missed the boat!" Oh, that Harry! What a card!

He looked across the aisle at a man graying at the temples. Too bad about him. He had a drinking problem. He hoped the man was listening to the sermon on moderation. He could use it. But maybe the preacher could use it too. The sermon was getting a bit immoderate in length. Was the oven at home really off? He returned to his reverie.

Mentally he started working on the new season's program for the club. He had done some Bible research already and was considering Belshazzar's feast, the parable of the rich man and Lazarus, and those Corinthians who had turned the Lord's Supper into a shambles. All three offered some real menu pos-sibilities. He already had a title for the last one. "Corinthian Cuisine"! He couldn't decide on the others. What about Fettuccine Alfredo or Beef Wellington? His mouth watered. All sorts of dishes passed through his head, if not his stomach. Selle de Venison, Filet de Boeuf Pique Richelieu, Perdreau Aux Ananas. Or how about Grab Meat Ravigote? Somewhere in the season ahead he simply had to include Souffle de Scampi Chablisienne and Noisettes d'Agneau Henri. Did the Bible say anything about Russia? He hoped so. He'd like to work in some Beef Stroganoff some time, not to mention Chicken Kiev and Shaslyk. The elder in front of him seemed intent on the sermon. Last week the elder had asked him why he didn't come to evening services as regularly as in the past. He had told him that he didn't feel the necessity of attending church twice on Sunday. After all, there was such a thing as being spiritually overfed. He didn't need that much religious sustenance. Why risk spiritual indigestion? Did Paul ever really go to Spain? He would research that. Nice if he did. It would make another menu possible for one of the meetings. Banderilla of Prawns Español, Brochette of Filet Mignon Cortes, Beef Madeira. Sangria would be a good wine, topped off with Flaming Coffee Español.

He checked his bulletin and noticed an announcement about the annual prayer day service for crops next Wednesday. He had forgotten about it. He and his wife had made a dinner date with some friends. Too late to cancel now. They were going to an expensive restaurant that would probably set him back fifty bucks. Better go light on lunch that day. A bagel, yogurt, and fruit would tide him over.

He found a dollar in his pocket for the special collection after the sermon was finally finished. When the minister announced that the offering was for the Christian Reformed World Relief Committee's program to feed the hungry, his hand went into his pocket again. He came up with another dollar. Why not? It was for a good cause.

After the service he raced home. The oven was on. The pot roast was simmering.

It smelled like heaven.

space trilogy
for advent

Chapter Thirty

I. The Captain

Over a hundred years ago, around the 1970s, people sometimes described their flea-hops to the moon as giant steps. Imagine! They spoke of having entered the "Space Age." Presumptuous! They often referred to planet Earth as their "spaceship." How quaint! The limitations of their imaginations were equaled only by the limitations of their accomplishments. For, though they spoke of light-years, and more, they little understood the immeasurability of the cosmos in which they lived.

The earth a spaceship? Hardly! The metaphor, acceptable then, is unacceptable now. Today, instead of speaking of "Spaceship Earth," we think, at least, in terms of "Spaceship Solar System." Even this hardly does justice to the surrounding vastness. In this Spaceship Solar System, the sun is the engine, the planets and satellites the structural parts, and Earth is the crowded but habitable cabin. Angels are the crew.

Like hijackings of a century ago, an evil angel tried to take over the controls soon after Spaceship Solar System took off. This created intolerable conditions in the cabin. The passengers became his slaves and hostages and each other's enemies. Misery abounded.

What happened is a wonder. Even under the most powerful cosmic microscope, Spaceship Solar System is hardly visible, to say nothing of its cabin and its occupants. Even so, the Creator cared enough to send his Son to wrest the control of this smallest of spaceships from the hands of the evil angel. How the Son of God boarded Spaceship Solar System is one of the greatest of all miracles and is celebrated every December 25. Today, he is the Captain. Some bombs are still aboard. But the word on intercom is reassuring, even though we are told the cabin will eventually burn. Those who trust their Captain will know him as their pilot for eternity in a new spaceship called "the new heaven and earth."

II. The Flower

In the last century, the people of a small European country told each other the story of the flower. Once upon a time, in the spring of a new year, a tiny green sprout stuck its head through the soil. It grew into a sturdy plant. The sun and rain were gracious; soon a bud appeared, and then the flower.

Time went by, and the flower bloomed, feeling glorious and strong. But a day came when it grew dissatisfied, for the temperature was too low. The flower thought about it, developed some ideas, and issued a statement. "Earth stands too far from the sun," it said. "That's why it is so cold. If the sun would come nearer, it would be warmer. The distance is too great."

The days passed, and the flower forgot its criticism. But a week later it became too warm. It was hot. Again the flower was dissatisfied. After thinking and reflecting, it made another statement. "Earth stands too near the Sun," it said. "That's why it is so hot. If the sun would move farther away, it would be cooler." The flower forgot that it was contradicting its statement of a few days earlier, but it could hardly be blamed for its inconsistency. After all, it was only a flower.

But what about people? They often register similar complaints. Those who believe that God is too far away feel neglected. Those who complain that he is too near wish that he would leave them alone. Which is right? Is God too high up or too near? The answer lies in the distance between the sun and its planet Earth. That distance is just right to prosper human life. So God. He is far enough from us to insure his holiness; high enough so that nothing is higher; distant enough to shine over all. At the same time he is as near as sunlight to the sod. The distance is just right. To live, people need both God's transcendence and God's presence. The latter finds expression in Emmanuel—God with us—Christmas.

III. The Prodigal

He was tired of the whole scene. He had said, "Father, give me the spacecraft that is my inheritance so that I can get away from it all." He had just taken off. Earth was receding. He went to 40,000 and then to 120,000 feet. Cruising briefly at that level, he felt a little frightened. But only momentarily. He shifted to the speed of light and found himself among the stars.

How peaceful he felt! How detached! He felt powerful, godlike. Time stood still. His body required no sustenance. Best of all, he had escaped from troubled Earth. That miserable planet was out of sight. And gone with it, his whole miserable existence upon it.

A face registered on the screen. A face, billions of miles from Earth? Miraculous communication followed through extrasensory perception. The stranger among the galaxies urged him to return to Earth. "You are needed there," he said.

As one galaxy faded and another appeared, he answered. "Return to Earth? Why should I exchange my present serenity and tranquillity for the pain of living on a fleck? Who in his right mind would substitute the glories of space for the narrowness of Earth, and Star Peace for world wars?"

"I did," said the face, thereby revealed his identity. The Prodigal remembered. He thought of Christmas and its meaning. Peering ahead into the depths of space, powdered with stars, he pondered.

He turned to the ship's computer and set his course for Earth.

nothing sacred

Chapter Thirty-One

Once upon a time lived a beauteous young maiden who was looking for her Prince Charming. Prince Charming was on his pinto looking everywhere for his beauteous young maiden. When they met, they fell in love and knew at once that they would marry and live happily ever after. He proposed. She accepted and set a date.

The maiden, who had always dreamed of being married in the air-conditioned Chapel of the Eternal Flame, took to her bed and fumed, face to the wall, when she learned that another wedding was already scheduled in the chapel on her chosen day. The maiden's mother thereupon persuaded the maiden's father to "do something," which he did. For an additional fee, an adjustment was made that brought happiness to all concerned. The wedding would take place on the Saturday in question, after all, and in the air-conditioned Chapel of the

Eternal Flame! As the father said, "Nothing is too good for my sweet baby."

The guidebook for weddings said that tradition suggested the pastor of the bride (if she had one) as the officiating clergyman, rather than the pastor of the groom (if he had one). But what if the pastor of the bride was clearly too short? His lack of stature would spoil the wedding picture! The community's most prestigious photography studio, "The Dark Room," was telephoned and asked to shed some light on this problem. The girl at the other end of the line had quick answers. "Whenever we use him" (referring to the bride's pastor), "we put him on a soapbox. Draped. The soapbox, I mean." It seemed a measure to complement his character as well as his lack of height.

In the light of all this, they contacted and engaged the groom's clergyman. He was relieved that the event was planned for the Chapel of the Eternal Flame and for a Saturday some months hence. He should be well by then. His last three weddings had been hard on him. One had been under water, another on horseback, and a third had been a hurried reading of an abbreviated formulary uniting two sky divers. The whole thing had taken place high above the Chapel of the Eternal Flame while plummeting earthward. Too bad the groom had dropped the ring! This would be an easier wedding. All that was required for the ceremony was a reading, with guitar accompaniment, from *The Wisdom of the Seer* ("there are no parking places on the highway of life"); the vows (memorized and spoken in tongues); and the sevenfold amen (flute only).

The guest list was a headache and caused arguments. Her relatives and his, her friends and his, her parents' friends and his parents' friends—their total far exceeded the bride's father's financial capacity. The bride, furthermore, wanted the wedding dinner at the "Eat, Drink, and Be Merry," which was a new barn built by the late owner of the old one. It came complete with bar and orchestra. Together with the price of the gowns, the whopping florist bill, the food, and the booze, the father bravely contemplated an astronomical sum as he swallowed his martini hard and said, "Nothing is too good for my sweet baby!"

The premarital conference with the clergyman turned out to be far more congenial than had been anticipated. The Reverend Father was seated behind his study desk with one foot elevated and bandaged. He had just conducted a barefooted wedding by the edge of Paradise Lake, with readings from Tennyson (the bride was English) and Emerson (the groom was American). A passing snake had bitten the good Reverend's toe while he was reading Tennyson. What a sense of humor that fellow had! "Maybe snakes can't talk, but they surely can object to English poetry! It would have been far better to read from *The Seer,*" he said. He especially liked that profound line: "There are no parking places on the highway of life."

The rehearsal was a shambles, which according to the minister was a good sign. It meant that the wedding itself would be a success. The groom's father was unhappy with the cost of the rehearsal dinner. The bride's father was unhappy that the groom's father was getting off so cheap. The mothers, already exhausted and facing an unnerving day filled with visits to the hairdresser and other last-minute duties, were smiling outwardly and screaming inwardly. The beauteous young maiden was mad at Prince Charming for being late and for not having memorized his lines. The organist was bored, having to play the processional too many times, and the clergyman was eager to get home in order to put his toe in Epsom salts.

The wedding was a triumph in staging. A Hollywood director could not have improved on anything. The photographer, who would also get a healthy slice of the wallet of the bride's father, clicked away to preserve this extravaganza, in color, for posterity. This was a scene right out of heaven. Women reached for their handkerchiefs right there in the Chapel of the Eternal Flame!

Recessional. Reception line. The dinner. The slicing of the cake, after which the bride and groom slipped away for a honeymoon in Hawaii. They returned to settle down to a married life with a statistical 30 percent chance of success.

Alas, the Eternal Flame flickered and died! The father of the beauteous young maiden engaged the best lawyer in town. "After all," he said, "nothing is too good for my sweet baby!"

keeping up

Chapter Thirty-Two

Once upon a time there was a minister. He served the Church by the Side of the Road.

He was no orator, but he delivered good sermons. He preached the Bible and the catechism. He preached the gospel of Jesus Christ.

The church was filled every Sunday. So were the offering plates. The membership roll was increasing. So were the activities. Everything was growing, including his son, who also wanted to become a preacher.

When the son was old enough, the minister sent him to the great School of Divinity in the big city. Tuition was almost more than the minister could afford, but famous teachers taught there. He wanted his son to have the best available theological training. He also wanted his son to share his learning by way of

131

letters. This way, his own ministry would improve. The congregation would profit.

The minister doubled his efforts as pastor of the Church by the Side of the Road. With his son following in his footsteps, he had an added incentive. And the church continued to be filled every Sunday, as well as the offering plates. The membership roll was still growing. So were the activities.

After a time, the minister received a long letter from his son. It contained a surprise. The letter said that the church was in a bad way. Attendance was down everywhere. Collections were getting smaller. Membership rolls were diminishing. So were the activities.

The minister read on. The son wrote that the church needed new approaches to worship. New liturgies had to be devised. Creative variations needed to be introduced. Innovations would stay receding tides.

The minister was as grateful as he was surprised to receive this information, together with some specific suggestions. Soon thereafter he began to practice some of them. A few were definite improvements. He was glad to notice that the pews and offering plates were still being filled. He was happy that the membership roll was still growing, though at a smaller rate. So were the activities.

Many months went by. The son was too busy to write. When he finally sent another letter, it told more discouraging tidings. The church, despite innovations, was still in a bad way. Attendance was down everywhere. Collections were getting even smaller. Membership rolls were diminishing. So were the activities.

The letter continued. The son said that a new approach to Genesis was needed, as was a whole new method of interpreting Scripture. It was called the "new hermeneutics." This was another kind of age. These were radically different times. Frank reappraisals of the Bible were long overdue. The eternal in the sacred pages had to be separated in new ways from the temporal and the cultural.

The minister read on. He appreciated his son's concern for the diminishing church. The letter said that Christianity could only turn the corner if its pulpits viewed the Bible less as revelation and more as a witness to revelation. The church also needed new theology of missions, one that would take more account of a pluriform society and the kind of ecumenism that would wrench us loose from the seventeenth century. The letter further touched on the field of ethics, in which situations were so very determinative.

The minister was grateful for this information. It was so fine of his son to put him in touch with the latest wisdom and suggest some books. He ordered a few and read them. Obviously he needed to alter some of his views.

A few Sundays later, the congregation noticed a new note in the minister's sermons, expressing some alien ideas and buttressed by quotations from leading world-renowned churchmen. It was obvious that the pastor was not standing still. It was so obvious that, though he was the minister of the Church by the Side of the Road, he was not, theologically, going to be left by the side of the road. But the church was emptier than before. The membership roll was, in fact, decreasing. So were the activities.

The next letter from his son was longer still. And the news was just as bad. The churches were having hard times. Attendance was a growing problem. Collections were minute. So were the activities.

A new theory of the atonement was the answer. The substitutionary aspect of that doctrine had to be replaced. It focused too much on God's justice rather than his love. Obviously the resurrection event would have to be reinterpreted. It may have been basic for Pauline theology. But today the empty tomb as the great nonhistorical reality needed to be emphasized. The minister was impressed.

The following Sunday, he addressed the deity in the congregational prayer as "Great and Almighty Ground of All Being." But fewer listeners were in the pews.

Time went on. The son received his doctorate. His thesis was entitled "The Beneficial Byproducts of Theological Tolerance." When he came home, the father arranged to have his son preach the sermon the following Sunday. It was going to be all about a new gospel for a new age.

It was a proud moment for the father. During the prelude, they proceeded together down the aisle and seated themselves in the pulpit chairs. The sanctuary was one-quarter filled. As the minister surveyed the few faces, he whispered to his son.

"Son, you were entirely right. You can see it for yourself. Attendance is down. Collections are getting smaller. The membership roll is diminishing. So are the activities."

fabrication

Chapter Thirty-Three

I am seeking a friendly lady who belongs to a wire-haired terrier. I owe her an abject apology.

It all began, innocently enough, with Dick and Judy going away and leaving their dog in our care. Shadow is friendly, obedient, and very Christian. At least, when the Bible is read for devotions, at table, she lies respectfully still. She is also a good walking companion and arresting in appearance. People especially notice her long hair. Like a 1947 Studebaker, they cannot tell her front from her rear.

Each morning and evening we looked forward to our walks together, disagreeing only on where she could leave her calling cards. With her hairy face and eyes completely hidden, I felt a little like a seeing-eye man. Still, it was Shadow who spotted the terrier and the friendly woman at the other end of its leash.

"Hi," she called, smiling from across the street. It is wonderful, I thought, how easily dog owners converse. With canine icebreakers, they are unlike ships that pass in the night. I read of a fellow once who "rented" a dog just so he could meet the young lady in the park where, each evening, she walked her own. And I remember two preachers who were on no speaking terms whatsoever. Having split a theological hair, they had joined opposing camps and become enemies. They knew they'd never speak again. But one morning, walking their dogs, they met. It was not the first time that tables were turned, in that a dog got a man to speak; indeed, two dogs got two men to speak, rather than bark at one another. Surely a dog is a man's best friend!

"Hi yourself!" I was equally cordial to the friendly woman who was now following her dog in my direction. "What kind of dog is that?" She addressed me as if we were old friends.

I was about to say that Shadow was a mixture, which, indeed, she is. She came from Tobermory, Canada—supposedly an Old English sheep dog. When it became apparent, as she grew, that she had other blood in her—something having gone unaccountably awry, as her breeders said—Dick and Judy had their money cheerfully refunded. Before I could answer, however, Friendly Lady spoke again. "I've been watching your dog for a block and I can tell, even by the walk, that she is a purebred and though I say it myself, I'm never wrong."

I couldn't contradict Friendly Lady and tell her that she was, in fact, dead wrong; Shadow was a mutt. So I simply said, "Sheep dog." I said it proudly. It was really no lie, I thought. It was, indeed, half true. Yet, this was my mistake. The rest of the conversation was all downhill for me.

"But it's not an Old English. I can tell by the plume of the tail!"

So she did know her dogs! What was I to say next! The whole truth? But that would certainly deflate Friendly Lady! She was so nice—so self-assured! Amazing how many thoughts can flow through the brain in a split second.

In the following split second, I spoke. "You're right! Not Old English! She's a Shropshire sheep dog." Where that word *Shropshire* came from so fast I haven't the foggiest, unless the devil put it on my tongue. It was an English word, and it sounded just right. I repeated it again, meanwhile wondering where Shropshire was, if, indeed, it was a place at all.

Friendly Lady was delighted. "I just knew it wasn't Old English, though I was sure it was a purebred. But I must confess I never knew Shropshires. Thank you for telling me."

"Not at all," I said, quite miserable by this time. Then, unaccountably and quite unnecessarily, I dug the hole still deeper. "You can always tell a Shropshire by the plume of its tail and by its friendly disposition." At this, Shadow fumed and glared at me with hidden eyes.

The next day we walked around a different block.

I wish to make amends. If you read this, friendly lady, forgive me. I made the same mistake Abraham made when he told Abimelech that his wife was his sister. What he said, like what I said, was half true because she was his "half" sister (Gen. 20:12). But half-truths always become whole lies. Preachers, too, like the father of believers, need to remember that they must tell the truth, the whole truth, and nothing but the truth, not only in courtrooms, but on streets.

And in their pulpits too.

exegesis

Chapter Thirty-Four

It was his first preaching assignment. He was armed with his class sermon, the only one he had. His text, from the book of Hezekiah, was well known: "Three blind mice. See how they run. They all run after the farmer's wife. She cut off their tails with a carving knife. Did you ever see such a sight in your life as three blind mice?" He had worked hard on reducing his text to its proper theme and three required divisions. As follows:

MOUSE BLINDNESS
I   Its Deplorable Extent
II Its Consequent Confusion
III Its Tragic Result

After the service he felt he had done fairly well. In his first point ("Its Deplorable Extent"), he had shown how a sightless condition had been found in not one, nor even two, but in three small rodents, a not inconsiderable number. In his second point ("Its Consequent Confusion"), he had demonstrated how this blindness had resulted in a rather ludicrous pursuit. Had the mice been able to see, they would probably have given chase to a piece of cheese or something similar. But certainly not to Homo sapiens. He had, in his third and final point ("Its Tragic Result"), elaborated on how a deplorable condition, issuing forth into a confused pursuit, had culminated in disfigurement and tragedy.

After the service, the vice president of the consistory took him aside. As a man who had made his own rather considerable study of the book of Hezekiah, he thought that the young seminarian had missed the central thrust of the passage. "Obviously," he said, "this verse is really about the activity of running and not about the condition of blindness. Surely, the key phrase is 'see how they run.'"

The seminarian saw the point. He was not unwilling to learn. Accordingly, he reworked his entire sermon for his next preaching assignment, which was the following week in another town. After reading the passage, and after a brief introduction, he announced his theme and points. As follows:

MICKEY AND HIS FRIENDS
I   Their Boundless Exuberance
II Their Dubious Objective
III Their Surprise Bonus

In his first point ("Their Boundless Exuberance"), he pointed out that Mickey and his friends so loved running that nothing, not even blindness, could stop them. In his second point ("Their Dubious Objective"), he explained that Mickey and his friends loved running so much that they would chase anything, even Homo sapiens. (He couldn't resist working in some Latin again.) And in his third point ("Their Surprise Bonus"), he sought to show how, unencumbered by tails in the end, Mickey and his friends were thereby enabled to run all the more freely and joyfully.

After the service, a member of the congregation, who was also president of the town's Anti-Everything Society, approached him. Wearing a disapproving look, this man wanted to know what in the world they were teaching in seminary these days. Having studied the passage preached, he was sure that its message was not about the joys of running, but, rather, that evil pursuit brings pain in the end.

The seminarian was discouraged. He had done his best, and now he had to change his message again. After all, the president of the Anti-Everything Society had a point. This preaching business was harder than he thought. He was convinced that he should profit from this new insight and remodel his sermon a third time before preaching it again the following Sunday in a third town. When the day arrived, he read the same passage as before but announced a different theme and points. As follows:

THE SPIRIT OF THE AGE
I   It Is Everywhere
II   It Is Marked by Sex and Violence
III It Is Unparalleled in History

In his first point ("It Is Everywhere"), he showed how much deplorable "running around" goes on, even in the country. Nor is it limited to mice. Homo sapiens run around plenty too! In his second point ("It Is Marked by Sex and Violence"), he dwelt on the scandal of the object of pursuit being one who was married, and how even kitchen utensils, such as carving knives, are used for weapons. In his concluding point ("It Is Unparalleled in History"), he pointed dramatically, for proof, to the words "Did you ever see such a sight in your life?" After the service, an emeritus minister phoned him to tell him that he had missed the boat. He had preached on the passage years before, and this text dealt with the root of all evil. The retired cleric recalled his own theme and points. As follows:

THE LOVE OF MONEY
I   It Coarsens Even the Finest
II   It Preys Even on the Helpless
III It Always Results in Loss

In his first point ("It Coarsens Even the Finest"), he said he had shown how profits from the sale of mice tails were so strong a temptation that it had transformed a farmer's wife into a knife-wielding maniac who had engineered the whole encounter in the first place. In his second point ("It Preys Even on the Helpless"), he had told his congregation how a love for profit will not hesitate victimizing even the blind. And in his last point ("It Always Results in Loss"), he had shown how there is no profit without loss, for three mice had ended up short. "The whole passage," said the retired minister, "is a tale that is told of tails that are sold. For money!"

The seminarian sighed. He thanked his caller and hung up the phone.

It was obvious he still had a lot to learn.

forgive us

Chapter Thirty-Five

Marty and Johnny were great friends. They went to the same country school by the great pasture and played at each other's houses. They played cops and robbers, mountain climbers, and spacemen.

One day they grew tired of playing cops and robbers, mountain climbers, and spacemen. They asked their parents what else they could do. One of them said that when they were younger they played "church" a lot. This seemed a good idea. So Marty and Johnny played "church." That's when all the trouble started.

Both wanted to be the minister. Marty won the argument because he was bigger. He was the head minister. Johnny, however, could preach the sermon because he earned better marks on his report card. First Marty and Johnny prayed the Lord's

Prayer together. Marty said, "and forgive us our trespasses."
Johnny said, "and forgive us our debts."

They didn't get any further into the prayer. Instead, they
stopped and argued more than before. Marty said it was wrong
to say "debts." Johnny said it was wrong to say "trespasses."
Finally, Marty hit Johnny. Johnny hit Marty. They separated.
Each went home and played church all by himself.

The next day they told all their friends at school. Marty said
it was proper to say "trespasses." Johnny claimed it was a
downright sin to say anything but "debts." Both were most rigid
in their positions. Some agreed with Marty; some agreed with
Johnny. Others didn't care.

Marty gathered together all those who agreed with him.
Johnny took the names of those on his side. Both tried to enlist
those who had not made up their minds or who didn't care.

The followers of Marty called themselves *Trespasstarians*.
Johnny's associates called themselves *Debtorarians*. The Trespasstarians perceived themselves superior to the Debtorarians.
The Debtorarians, in turn, looked down their noses at the
Trespasstarians. At noon recess, they divided the playground.
Neither would play with the other. For a Trespasstarian to tres-
pass into Debtorarian territory was a hazardous move. And it
became equally dangerous for a Debtorarian to retrieve a ball
from Trespasstarian ground.

Soon neither group played ball anymore. It was less fun than
before, when they were all together. Anyway, they were onto
more serious business. Both groups had to organize themselves. One weak Debtorarian was caught conversing with an
indifferent Trespasstarian. This made it necessary for the
Debtorarians to form an anti-Trespasstarian committee. Their
job was to warn all Debtorarians against the evils of Trespass-
tarianism. The Trespasstarians did likewise. They formed a
committee to watch for any Debtorarianistic tendencies in the
group. More organization followed. Each group developed

levels of authority and rule books. No one could go directly to Marty with a matter. No one could go directly to Johnny. They had to observe proper channels.

Billy came from a neighboring village. He had heard about the separation of his friends. He wanted to bring them together. He said that if they could compromise and pray "forgive us our sins," they could be friends again as before. Both Marty and Johnny proved that this could not be. Both remained firm. Neither of them wanted to be known as Sinnerarians. And anyway, the Trespasstarians and the Debtorarians had grown too far apart in other ways. Marty used a big word. He said Billy's suggestion was not feasible. Johnny used big words too. He said Billy's plan, though substantive, was nonetheless unrealistic.

One day a sheep from the great pasture wandered into Trespasstarian territory. The Debtorarians were jealous. They put out some nice food that night to entice the sheep into their own territory. When this worked, they quickly advertised their membership statistics as having increased by one. The Trespasstarians mirrored this tactic. Sheep stealing became a priority in both camps.

One day a Trespasstarian noticed a lamb missing. He notified the proper committee immediately. The committee had just adjourned. At their next meeting, a week later, they made the lost lamb their first item on a lengthy agenda. Unanimously, committee members placed the lamb question into the hands of a searcher. The latter, needing data, communicated immediately with the "Division on Lambs." He sent a questionnaire to determine such matters as weight, age, and further pertinent statistics. Since the "Division on Lambs" was closed for the Easter holidays, no immediate reply was possible.

While awaiting word, the searcher also communicated with his counterpart in the camp of the Debtorarians. Perhaps they could cooperate in so important a matter. The latter replied that a joint search was inconceivable. He wrote that though a lamb was important, the question of how to pray the fifth petition of the Lord's Prayer took precedence and had first to be resolved. He added that, because both were so firm in their positions, cooperation was unlikely, even on so important a matter as a lost lamb.

When the bell rang that afternoon, calling all the children in from play, the teacher showed them some bones. He said they were lamb bones. He had found them on the broad road that led past the school.

Prayer: "Sometimes, Lord, help us to back down from firm positions. And when, because of its follies and imperfections, we sometimes feel inclined to give up on the church, remind us that you never do. Amen."

the daze of our years

Chapter Thirty-Six

The catechism class was in revolt. True, they were not unruly or discourteous. Quite the contrary. They were giving their teacher their full attention. What he said, however, met with strong disagreement. They simply could not accept the teaching that God worked all things for good for his children.

"What about Mrs. Brown?" they asked. "Why was she widowed with three small children? Instead of taking her husband, why didn't God take Mr. Smith—the oldest member in the congregation, ninety-eight, and ready and willing to go?"

This was an intelligent class of youngsters. They easily buttressed their point with further illustrations. God's ways seemed erratic, even irrational. One of them knew a little about Psalm 73, though he got the numbers turned around. Something about the "wicked flourishing." "It doesn't make sense," he said; then he added, "The riddle of life leaves me in a daze."

The teacher let them talk. When he had listened long enough, he waved his hand for silence. "Follow me," he said, and disappeared into the closet.

Puzzled, the twelve class members stepped into the small enclosure. They saw some shelves holding a few old coverless Bibles, a gavel, some hymnbooks, and a small volume by C. S. Lewis. Hearing their teacher's voice from the back, they pushed through a rack of choir robes and landed on a wide, busy street.

"This is the Avenue of Life," he said. "Let's take a walk"— whereupon he led his small entourage across the street to a church whose construction was nearing completion. Once inside, they headed for the sanctuary, which was finished except for the painting.

The place was worshipful. Especially attractive were the free-standing columns along the outer aisles. Made of wood, they were unpainted, giving them a fresh and natural look. An interior decorator bustled about, mixing colors and directing the several painters. The button he wore on his lapel read, "Quiet. Genius at work."

One of the young people cried out in dismay. The painter had begun painting the front column an ugly dark color, completely obliterating that fresh and natural look. What a shame! They left the church mumbling remarks something less than complimentary.

Back on the street again, the catechism class, led by their shepherd, walked for several blocks. A smiling cook in the window of a restaurant was preparing the "special" for the day. Obviously someone was making a killing on buttons, for he wore the same one sported by Mr. Interior Decorator. But what a mishmash. Watching the man mixing vegetables and meats that didn't belong together, the class decided that he wasn't that great in the kitchen. The teacher agreed. He said that he preferred home cooking to whatever that guy was making. And so, having rendered their corporate judgment, the thirteen progressed to a stop many blocks later. There, on a corner, a man had set up his easel, preparing to paint the scene before him. With no small curiosity, they looked over his shoulder and thus missed seeing the same button that had brightened the chests of the decorator and the cook.

The group was disillusioned. The artist was obviously no Rembrandt. Though they observed him for more than an hour, they could make no sense of what they saw on his canvas.

A mile further they stopped again at a pottery place. "Another genius at work," laughed one in the group, spying a button on a man who had just taken up a raw lump of clay. After watching for a while, one of the girls, who made pots for a hobby, announced that the man was doing it all wrong. The others, including the teacher (all self-styled experts by this time), readily expressed the same opinion. Whatever the man had in mind, the results could be nothing but ugly. Thus they all left to sit in a park.

The boys, after running and cavorting on the grass, decided that they were hungry. The teacher decided that he would take them to that very restaurant they had visited.

On the way back, in the window of the pottery shop they noticed a vase—the very one they had seen in the making. It was beautiful! Farther up the street, the artist was putting the finishing touches on his painting. It was absolutely gorgeous! At the restaurant, all ordered the special, which was so delicious they all wanted more. Stuffed, they went back to the church they had visited. The columns were now painted with so dark a color they looked almost black. Each one looked so strong and powerful that all revised their earlier opinion of the decorator upwards. Finally, tired and gladdened, they pushed through the closet again.

"What have we learned today?" asked the teacher. Without waiting for answers, he provided his own. "I learned," he said, "that we can never judge the product at any point in the process. I also learned that we can never judge the artist at any point in his work. We must always await the result." When all agreed, he asked, "Does anyone see a connection here between all of this and Mrs. Brown, whose husband, in our opinion, died untimely? Or old Mr. Smith, who lives when some of us might think that he should have been taken instead of Mr. Brown? And what about those 'flourishing wicked' in Psalm 73?"

The boy who had said that life is a riddle looked up. "I'm less in a daze now," he said. The teacher smiled. "God is a cook," he observed, "and a potter, an artist, an interior decorator, and everything else rolled into one." Then he asked them all to write down this sentence:

"Only with God does the end always justify the means."

After prayer, one girl had an afterthought: "What about those buttons saying 'Quiet. Genius at work'?"

"Oh, that," said the minister. "It's a text out of the Bible. It's found in Psalm 46:10." They all looked it up at home that night: "Be still and know that I am God."

the blahs

Chapter Thirty-Seven

Dear Pastor or Consistory:

This form letter is no junk mail. You might read it and save a church—your own!

Has attendance at your small groups fallen off? Has it become harder to get men and women involved in Bible study? Has the steering committee lessened its drive? Are the young people losing interest? Do the pews have fewer occupants on Sunday mornings or evenings or both?

Perhaps your congregation is flourishing in every way. If so, your church is the exception and has no need of our organization. If, on the other hand, your responses to these questions are in the affirmative, your ecclesiastical organization has "the blahs."

This is where we enter the picture. Our experts have been trained to give you the assistance we think you need. Consider the following testimonial from our files:

We are a church on the east coast with a long and useful history. In the last decade, however, we have experienced a falling away of the membership, despite updating our theology. We have banished such concepts as sin, sanctification, and other notions associated with the old-time religion. Nevertheless, our congregational life had lessened in vitality.

We contacted you for help. Pastor Blob immediately arranged to conduct a Sunday evening service. His approach was unique. When he came to 'the sermon' in our liturgy, he closed the Bible and told the handful of parishioners that we would play a game of 'Trust' instead. He divided us into leaders and followers. The followers were blindfolded while the leaders led them up and down the aisles and through the narthex and the nave. After fifteen minutes the roles were reversed.

Only one worshiper reacted negatively—an old elder who speculated that Blob stood for "Blind Leader of the Blind." All the others felt that the body contact (holding hands) and the exercise of faith in their leaders was a most uplifting experience. One of our middle-aged women, who had been led by Pastor Blob personally, said that she had received more out of the service than any she could remember in the last ten years. We are eagerly looking forward to what he will do next Sunday, and we expect a bigger crowd.

This is but one of many letters recommending our organization.

Our expertise is by no means limited to revitalizing worship services through new concepts and restructurization. We are prepared to advise on all aspects of congregational activities, concentrating especially on societies and clubs gone stale and in need of new formats. A small sample from our "things to do for church societies" indicates our creativity in this area.

Feeling the Church—Begin with light refreshments. Upon the leader's instructions, let all walk around the entire church, touching the bricks, the siding, the windows, the doors, and so on, taking note of surface textures, solidity, and the like. Participants should reach as high as they can and feel the church at mid- and ground-level. Reassemble. Discuss feelings and sensations. Finish with more light refreshments.

Note: In urban areas, notify the police department in advance of this activity to avoid and possible complications.

Here's Looking at You—Instruct everyone, via a bulletin announcement, to bring binoculars to the meeting. Sit in a large circle. Let each one present stare at length at each other person through the wrong end of the binoculars. Encourage all to move about in the room, continuing to gaze through the wrong end of the binoculars. At a signal from the leader, let all reverse binoculars, continuing to walk and stare at each other. Say "Aha!" Hold panel discussion for comparing reactions. Follow with refreshments.

Note: Those in urban areas are advised to draw the shades.

Falling Facades—Arrange chairs into groups of four. When all are seated, make animal sounds on signal from leader. Roar, squeak, sigh, yawn, gargle, and gasp. Feel vibrations. Discuss impressions and reactions. Refreshments.

The disciples were very close. We can help your groups reach the same togetherness through new ideas, replacing old Bible study formats.

So, does your church have the blahs? Write to Brotherly Love and Heterodox Services, Inc. (B.L.A.H.S.).

As we say around here, you can get rid of the small blahs by putting them in capital letters.

the circle of
our discontent

Chapter Thirty-Eight

It was time for the sermon to begin. The minister read from Philippians 4:11: "I have learned to be content whatever the circumstances." In the introduction he spoke of Paul, the author of these words. He pointed out that this statement was all the more remarkable coming from the pen of a man whose lot in life had been far from comfortable.

* * * * * * *

Johnny sat in the front row. His feet didn't quite touch the floor because he was only nine years old. He swung them because sitting still is very hard when you are young. And even though his parents had told him that it wasn't polite to turn around and stare at people behind him, he did so anyway. He wasn't disobedient, but remembering all the rules wasn't easy for anyone under ten. He saw Steve in the fourth row. That set him to thinking.

Steven was in college, and he was very tall. In fact, Steve was the star on the college basketball team. Only last Friday night Steve had scored thirty points. All of which made Johnny more than a little envious. Being only nine years old was hard! It would take forever to get to college where he too might shine someday on the basketball court. Before that he would have to finish grade school and high school, take hundreds of piano lessons, and probably have his teeth straightened. That would take forever! Johnny sighed as he turned to face forward once again.

He wished that he was Steve.

* * * * * * *

The minister had finished his introduction and began the first of his three points. He used the word *submit* a lot. "I submit to you," he said, "in the first place that contentment is a Christian art." He elaborated on the thought that this was a grace Christians had to learn through practice.

* * * * * * *

Steve, back there in the fourth row, had his mind on other things. Somehow, he couldn't get his thoughts on the sermon very well. Others, apparently, could. Mr. Sims, for example, seemed to be listening intently in the third row. Steve began thinking about Mr. Sims.

Mr. Sims was about forty-five years old and very successful in business. He had a good-looking wife and a son and daughter who had everything. He also owned a beautiful home and cottage and a brand-new expensive car in the church parking lot. And what a tan! The whole family looked like they had just come back from the South somewhere. Or maybe Hawaii. All

of which made Steve more than a little envious. Being in college was tough. Would he get a summer job this year? And what about grad school? How very long it would take for him to get to where Mr. Sims was! He had a long hard pull ahead. Steve sighed as he tried to tune in on the sermon again.
He wished that he was Mr. Sims.

* * * * * * *

The preacher was ready to submit a second point for the consideration of his hearers. He said that although contentment was an art that had to be developed, you couldn't develop what you didn't have. To have contentment, a person had to first have Christ. He began to cite Paul, among others, to illustrate his thought.

* * * * * * *

Mr. Sims, occupying his place in the third row, reached down and rubbed a scuff mark on one of his two-hundred-dollar shoes. Just then Mr. Hood, seated in front of him, put both his feet under his pew, toes down, revealing worn soles to Mr. Sims's eyes. It was enough to start a train of thought.

Mr. Hood was just a bit over sixty-five and retired. He went fishing a lot and grew the biggest and best roses on the block. His children were grown and on their own. His wife was well and active in the affairs of the church, together with her husband.

All of this made Mr. Sims more than a little envious. Staying ahead of the rat race wasn't easy. His responsibilities were a mile long, and his pressures weighed a ton. How nice it would be to be retired and able to take things a bit easier! Mr. Sims sighed as he forced his mind back on the sermon.

He wished that he was Mr. Hood.

* * * * * * *

Mr. Hood, in the second row, had listened well and fully agreed with everything he had heard. His attention, however, was occasionally interrupted by that restless boy in front of him. He knew little Johnny somewhat; he had given him a peppermint once or twice in the past. Fine lad. Good parents too. Mr. Hood fell to reminiscing. He remembered when he was that age. That was a long time ago. Life had been ahead of him then. Now it was mostly lived and gone. But it had been a good life. He'd suffered many knocks but experienced many blessings too. All the same, despite certain advantages of age, nearing the end of the line was kind of sad. He wouldn't mind living life all over again. Lots of exciting things were developing in God's plan and history, and he would just as soon be a part of it. Mr. Hood sighed as he closed his eyes for the final prayer.

He wished that he was Johnny.

oscar

Chapter Thirty-Nine

The Academy of Ecclesiastical Awards was holding its annual bash. All the nominees were present in their clerical attire, accompanied by wives wearing anxious smiles. Throughout the year, competition had been keen for the gold-plated Oscars made of zinc. Former recipients had discovered that these were, indeed, worth their weight in true gold in terms of calls, promotions, and the like. A few had even installed their trophies permanently and conspicuously in their pulpits. Saturday church ads identified various members of the cloth as "nominated for five academy awards," "winner of two academy awards," and so on.

Proceedings commenced sharply at 10 P.M., as previously arranged with the television network, which had promised to fit everyone in the picture. The orchestra opened with a mishmash of traditional and contemporary hymns, the organ and guitar taking turns with the melody. This nice touch was designed to satisfy all tastes.

The podium, naturally, looked like those of a pulpit. Magnificent carvings on three sides consisted of hundreds of little Oscars with wings. Some were blowing trumpets, oblivious of Matthew 6:2. Rev. Hope, instead of Reverends Faith and Love, served as Master of Ceremonies, because his name more successfully captured the nominees' moods. He was, furthermore, an M.E. (Master of Entertainment), a most impressive category in the world of ecclesiastical arts and sciences.

Dr. Preektoon pushed out four other nominees for "Best Achievement in Sound." His acceptance speech was characteristically much too long, though the droning of his words and sentences amply illustrated his worthiness of the honor he had won.

The "Best Achievement in Prayer" went to Dr. Flip, whose trousers were perfectly creased. And an Oscar for "Best Achievement in Illustration" was awarded to Rev. Inno Vate. In his acceptance speech, he thanked his supporting council, the members of which had dressed in various forms of fruit and cavorted in the chancel while he had preached a sermon on Galatians 5:22-23. He was a double winner, having also clinched "Best Achievement in Visual Effects" for having dressed up as a Bible for his sermon entitled "The Talking Book." The latter was also selected for inclusion in the prestigious *Homiletical Hits,* an annual volume of the year's best messages.

Dr. Terse's immense popularity was confirmed by the volume of applause that greeted his appearance. He received an Oscar for "Best Achievement in Short Subjects," having preached a two-and-a-half minute sermon. This topped the previous year's winner, who had been clocked at three minutes even. The "Best Documentary Award" went to Pastor Operator for his slide sermon on "The World's Best Beaches," with the musical background taken from the score of "Let the Lower Lights Be Burning."

"Best Performance by a Clergyman in a Supporting Role" was won by Ed Minister, who had held up the hands of his senior, a man who needed all the support he could get. Dr. A. Wonder captured the "Best Foreign Language Production"; his message, "The Simple Gospel," had contained 154 quotations from Latin, Greek, Hebrew, and Dutch, interspersed with a few English words, none of which had been less than five syllables in length.

"Best Supporting Performance by a Clergyman's Wife" went to Rev. Activist's spouse, who had spent 365 consecutive evenings alone without going to pieces. Rev. Inno Vate, already the possessor of two Oscars, won the category of "Best Achievement in Costume Design." Apparently he was outdistancing the field. This third award was for wearing appropriate and magnificent attire during the delivery of his monologue entitled "I Am Caesar."

Still more awards were presented for still more categories. "Best Achievement in (Bible) Editing," "Production of Best Bulletin," "Production of Best Liturgy," and so on. All nominees leaned forward to hear their own names called.

Then came the climax, the three biggest awards of all. "Best Performance by a Clergyman"—congratulations to U. Dickens Heep for his delivery of the sermon "The First Shall Be Last"! "Best Picture of the Year"—a huge finger painting secured the award for Rev. Inno Vate's Sunday school class. "Best Easter Extravaganza" (special category) was shared by Rev. Anne Athema for her development of the theme of "Spring" and Dr. Lucy for the moving sermon "If Jesus Had Survived His Cross."

What followed the supposed climax of the evening made the event most memorable, however. It was as unexpected as it was unscheduled. A stranger in shining garment strode from the wings of the stage. Instead of an Oscar, he carried a crown inscribed with the words "Well Done." The stranger explained that this award for the category "Achievement in Faithfulness" was to be given to literally hundreds upon hundreds, none of whom were present.

They were not present because they were being faithful in their studies and pulpits, visiting the sick, seeking the lost, comforting the sorrowing. And more.

versions

Chapter Forty

I am concerned about the increasing numbers of versions of the Truth.

A few years ago I walked into a catechism class carrying a stack of Bibles the length of my arms, all the way up to my chin. Respectfully depositing them on the desk, one on top of the other, I observed before the group that each section of that sacred tower represented a different translation of the Bible.

Inviting comments, I was particularly struck with the remark of a young woman. She thought it quite wonderful that people would spend so many hours studying the ancient languages in their efforts toward accuracy in presenting God's Word in English. Suddenly I felt a pang of remorse for having studied my Hebrew reluctantly so often in seminary days. I do not own a hat. But if I did, I would remove it in honor of those who patiently pore over ancient manuscripts and conjugations.

Their efforts are not what I have in mind when I express concern over the increasing numbers of versions of the Truth. True, their productions are adding to my sermon preparation time. After wrestling with a text in its original form, it was once my custom to consult King James and the version "set forth A.D. 1611, compared with the most ancient authorities and revised A.D. 1881-1885, and newly edited by the American Revision Committee, A.D. 1901." Now, I feel compelled to go further. I must now also consult the Revised Standard, the Berkeley, the Amplified, the New English, Jerusalem, Phillips, New International Version, and so on.

To say that this is my standard procedure would be dishonest. Reserving adequate time for sermon construction is actually a weekly struggle. But in my more conscientious moments, I now turn a lot of pages of a lot of Bibles, even one written in my ancestral tongue. Noting the nuances as they vary from volume to volume is instructive.

The King James still gives me the greatest satisfaction. This observation must please those who believe that *it* only is inspired and that God, "who spake at sundry times and in diverse manners," always did so in the style of Shakespeare. The truth is that the King James is not always the most accurate. Nor is its style easily grasped by a generation whose language has lost all style. I simply prefer it for personal reasons. I grew up with it.

To return from this digression, let me reiterate that my concern is not with those increasing numbers of versions, all of which strive for accuracy. It is rather with the increasing numbers of Orwellian versions that rewrite the Truth and that are expressed, if not on paper, in lives. Some say that none of the versions are inspired. This is not true. Those that bend or reshape the Truth definitely are inspired by the devil.

To illustrate such versions of the Truth as give me both pause and pain, allow me to attempt three modern renderings of

Psalm 23. The first might well stand as the Communist's Version, while the second is presented as the Materialist's Translation. No slur on Christian psychiatrists is intended with the third. It is the version of an alarming number who, despite high learning and modern sophistication, have no understanding of Psalm 8:4-5.

* * * * * * *

Karl Marx is my shepherd, I shall not want, eventually. He maketh me to lie. He leadeth me beside the truth. He restoreth all things to the state. He leadeth me in the paths of dialectics for Communism's sake. Yea, though I walk through the valley of the shadow of capitalism, I will not fear; for might is with me. The masses, they comfort me. Thou preparest a table before me laden with what belonged to others. Thou anointest my head with vision and determination. My cup will run over. Surely victory and all the world shall follow—eventually, and I will dwell in a Communist state *until I die.*

* * * * * * *

Ambition is my shepherd, I shall not want for anything, someday. It maketh me not to lie down. It leadeth me to greater effort. It restoreth my energies when I am tired. It leadeth me into such paths as will further and hurry my progress. Yea, though I walk through the valley of the shadow of reversal, I will not fear, but press on relentlessly, for the future is with me. The goal, the prize, success, they dazzle me. Thou preparest a table before me in a big mansion someday. Thou anointest my head with great determination; the possibilities run over. Surely wealth and position will be my lot for the rest of my days, and I will dwell in the gates of the city, honored and admired, *until I die.*

* * * * * * *

My psychiatrist is my shepherd, I shall not worry. She maketh me to lie down upon her couch. She leadeth me beside supportive, nondirective waters. She restoreth my self-love. She leadeth me into client-centered therapy for my psyche's sake. Yea, though I walk through scopophilial valleys and errogenous zones, I will fear no sin. For Freud is with me. His libido comforteth me. He prepareth pleasure centers in the presence of my retroactive inhibitions. He anointeth my Superego with sublimating conditioners. My self-esteem runneth over. Surely reinforcements and appointments with my psychiatrist shall follow me all the days of my life, and I shall dwell in the pursuit of self-actualization *until I die.*

any room?

Chapter Forty-One

Dear Readers:

I wish to thank your editor for giving me this page. I have long wished to communicate my thoughts to others, but I have never had the opportunity until now.

I am a hotel keeper. My name is not important. It could be John, or Hans, or Roberto. I have been in my kind of business for two thousand years. I could tell you quite a few stories, but there's only one that I must tell.

It was about two thousand years ago. I was running a small place in the little town of Bethlehem. It wasn't the Hilton. Small as it was, it was seldom filled, but on this occasion I could have rented closets. It was census time, and Caesar (Augustus, as I recall) wanted all citizens to register in the places of their birth. What a bonanza for me! I had people sleeping in the halls.

I remember especially one young fellow who came to me for a room. Quite an ordinary chap. I might have forgotten him except that his young wife was pregnant. I thought maybe somebody might be willing to give up his or her accommodations, seeing that the young lady appeared close to the time of her delivery. No one would. What could I do? The hotel business can be tough sometimes. I had to send them on their way. A few days later I heard that they found lodging in a stable, where the young lady gave birth to a healthy little boy.

I might have forgotten about it even then, except for what happened soon after. It was ghastly! Herod's soldiers came to town and put all male infants to the sword. They went through my hotel, room by room, and down the streets, house by house. You should have heard the weeping and the wailing that night! That's when I thought about that couple in the stable again. I found out that they had left town, just in time. My wife said, "Poor child, no room for him in our inn and no room for him in our town." I added, "And no room in the country," because they had gone to Egypt.

That became the story of his life. When they returned, they lived in Nazareth. But, just as with my hotel, and Bethlehem, and the country, Nazareth had no room for him. When he grew up and became a rabbi and preached for the first time in his home synagogue, he found that a prophet is without honor in his own country. What he said riled up the home folks so much that they led him to a hillside outside of town and tried to throw him down. And that's just about the way his whole ministry went.

One day he healed a man in the land of Gadara. He cast the devils out of him. They entered a herd of swine and destroyed the herd. The people were so incensed that they asked him to leave. No room in my hotel, Bethlehem, the country, Nazareth, Gadara—and so it went. He felt bad about it. He said that the foxes had holes, and the birds of the air had nests, but he had nowhere to lay his head.

The church had no room for him either: some of the leaders plotted his death. Nor did the government have room for him: Pilate didn't want him, and neither did Herod. And Jerusalem had no room for him. He was led outside its city gates to a place called Calvary. Indeed, it seemed that the whole world had no room for him, so they propelled him out of it on a cross.

You'd think that was the end of the story, but it wasn't. I've followed his case for two thousand years, and the "no room" signs have multiplied. No room for Jews, for Protestants, for Roman Catholics, for minorities. Religious wars, race wars, and such have stained all of history. Boiled down, it amounts to no room for him. When you do it to them (Jews, Protestants, Catholics, minorities, and others), you are really doing it to him.

But I must end. I said earlier that my name was not important. It could be John, or Hans, or Roberto. That was not true. Because, you see, my name is important, and it is John, and it is Hans, and Roberto. My name is your name, because you, too, are in the hotel business. Your hotel is your heart. He's at the door. He knocks. I hope you don't do what I did two thousand years ago and what so many have done down through the ages.

So, readers, I thank your editor again for this page. I hope everyone will read it. I've listened to some beautiful music during the Christmas season. One hymn is my favorite. The words go something like this: "O come to my heart, Lord Jesus. There's room in my heart for Thee."

I hope so.

I know one thing. There's room in his for you.

true story

Chapter Forty-Two

It was a fine church that sought to be faithful to God's Word and the confessional standards based on God's Word. It had a college and seminary in Grand Rapids, Michigan; a radio ministry based in Chicago; spent great sums of money on home and foreign missions and world relief. But like every other church, it was imperfect. It suffered from some factionalism, some doctrinal disputes, some negligence in the sphere of church discipline, and a few differences in further areas of Christian life and commitment. More than a few of its members offered suggestions about how their church could improve and come closer to where it ought to be.

Ideas were many and varied. What was needed was more spirituality. More prayer meetings would help. The church lacked warmth and emotion, especially in the worship services. They wanted members of the congregation to spontaneously call out some "amens" on occasion. They wanted more Holy Spirit, some Pentecostal fire, maybe even some speaking in tongues. "That will make us a better church and solve our problems," they said.

Others had a different notion. Equally concerned for the health and well-being of their church, they saw the solution in more doctrinal knowledge and understanding. They believed that increased and improved catechism classes were the answer. They insisted on more theological understanding, more Christian education, more instruction and training in the ways of God. "That will make us a better church and solve our problems," they said.

Still others had a third opinion. "When all is said and done, what is more important than faith?" they wondered. Surely, without faith it is impossible to please God. "Believe in the Lord Jesus, and you will be saved—you and your household." What was more important than that? In an age of unfaith, with many other churches losing what was once for all delivered unto the saints, more trust and confidence in God and his precious promises was the answer. "That will make us a better church and solve our problems," they said.

These three well articulated and ably defended points of view struggled not only among themselves for attention, but also with a fourth. This group sought a much greater spirit of stewardship and self-sacrifice. They decried the fact that so few tithed and gave only meagerly out of their abundance, remembering their obligations to God last. So much shining affluence parked in the church lot and so little in the collection plate was a shame. "The kind of giving that hurts—that will make us a better church and solve our problems," they said.

"More fervor!" said the first group. "More knowledge!" cried a second group. "More faith!" said a third. "More sacrifice!" demanded a fourth. And they argued among themselves. Some even developed hard feelings.

Then someone remembered that a missionary, centuries ago, had sent a letter to their church from across the seas. It addressed itself precisely to their situation. Each group gathered to hear it read, each faction expecting justification in distinction from the others. The missionary, who said he spoke for God—which indeed was true—said that all the groups were right. But he added that all of them were wrong as well.

Addressing himself to the first group, he said that more warmth was surely needed. "But," he added, "if you have such intense fervor and zeal that you can speak with tongues, and have not love, all you will be doing is making noise."

Directing himself to the second group, he said that more knowledge was an absolute must. "But," he added, "if you have so much knowledge that you understand all mysteries, and have not love, it will amount to nothing."

Looking at the third group, he said that more faith was desperately essential. "But," he added, "if you have enough faith to move mountains, and have not love, then faith minus love, like faith minus works, is dead."

Concentrating on the fourth group, he said more sacrifice was, indeed, necessary. "But," he added, "if you have such a spirit of sacrifice that you not only give all your goods to the poor, but also present your own bodies for burning, and have not love, nobody profits at all."

And so all four factions, realizing that increased zeal, knowledge, faith, and sacrifice were all essential, yet nothing without abiding love, added the ingredient without which they could not be a better church.

And so they became a better church.

an easter sermon

Chapter Forty-Three

Dear Congregation:

I propose a riddle. We have never met before, and we shall meet but once. Who am I?

I am one unloved, unsought, unsung. I bear the name "Grim Reaper." I am often depicted on canvas in the unflattering shape of the human skull. Sometimes I appear with a scythe, and in mythology I run a ferry boat on the River Styx.

I am Death!

Many on this earth try to camouflage my appearance or deny my existence. The Bible never speaks of me, however, as an illusion. Instead, it labels me the King of Terrors.

It tells the story of my birth in Paradise. "Conceived and born in sin," a phrase in one of your formularies, does not describe me. I was conceived *by* sin.

When I arrived, I reigned supreme. The whole earth was my domain. I wandered everywhere. No land escaped my coming and my staying. Little children were not immune to my touch, and even Methuselah did not elude my grasp. I fly through the night, as I did in Egypt when I claimed each firstborn child. I walk in the cool of the morning, as I did among the Assyrians in their camp. I often show my face unexpectedly, as I did to the man who filled his barns. Eve first saw my face when she looked on Abel lying on the ground.

True, I failed to touch a few lives in the distant past. Enoch walked beyond me. Elijah rose above my reach. These were the exceptions, though, not the rule.

A day came, however, that disturbed me greatly. A child was born in Bethlehem to deliver you from me. So the prophets said. I tried to capture him. Remember the massacre of the innocents? And that push on the top of a cliff in the vicinity of Nazareth? I failed both attempts. Meanwhile, my enemy succeeded in wresting three persons from my grasp: the daughter of Jairus, the son of the widow at Nain, and Lazarus, who had two sisters.

This child of Bethlehem and I came face to face. We met at Calvary in mortal combat. Some said I won. For a desperate few days, even his disciples were convinced of this. But when the sun rose, after the Sabbath had passed, the word flew. He is risen!

Some still say that I won and he lost. But I am here to tell you that he rose, that his resurrection is an incontrovertible truth, and that I lost the great struggle of Calvary.

Why, then, am I here? And why am I telling you all this? "What," you ask, "is Death doing in the pulpit?" T. S. Eliot spoke of murder in the cathedral. But what is Death doing in this cathedral? It is a good question. I am glad you ask.

I am here for the same reason you are here. I am here to praise his name, for I am a Christian now. I have been converted. Maybe you have forgotten this. If so, let me remind you of something. I am not only a convert—I am the very first convert to the Lord Jesus Christ! Many knees have bowed to him in two thousand years, but mine were the first. A whole week before Thomas said, "My Lord and my God," I spoke those famous words. I became my Lord's servant and, therefore, I am now your friend. I am a Christian. Surely you have heard of Christian Death.

I like your Heidelberg Catechism. I am particularly fond of Q&A 42: "Since, then, Christ died for us, why must we also die? Answer: Our death is not a satisfaction for our sins, but only a dying to sins and entering into eternal life." Surely, then, I am your friend! Paul viewed me as one. He said, "For me to live is Christ, and to die is gain."

So you see, I've changed my character, as every true convert should. Because I am in his service, you need not fear me anymore. I have lost my sting. Your own Bible says so. Praise the Lord! I am not eloquent. My nature is to be silent. But always, and especially on Easter, I sing to him as loud as anyone.

And so, dear friends—till we meet again. If Christ tarries, we will, without a doubt. We may meet in a sickroom or on a highway. We may meet in your house or right here in church. We do not know the time of our appointment. We shall leave that to my Lord and King. But since neither of us knows the time or place, I suggest you be ready now—by making sure that my King is your Lord as well.

I still have one characteristic from before Christ conquered me. When I met a man in the old days, I always took him alone, never his baggage. You would be surprised what people want to bring when I take their hand. The old Egyptian Pharaohs were a good case in point. They made sure that they were embalmed and entombed with plenty of gold and silver. Others want to take an armful of good works. I've seen them holding to shelves full of theological tomes. But he who travels with me travels light. Remember the play *You Can't Take It with You?*

It's true. When I bring you to your Lord, you come as you are.

But I must close. The Bible says something about being persuaded that death shall not separate us from the love of Christ. Not only do I not separate you from him, I bring you to him, if you are his.

Wonderful! Before you meet me, he is with you. After you meet me, you are with him.

i am joe's soul

Chapter Forty-Four

Some years ago *The Reader's Digest* featured an article entitled, "I Am Joe's Heart." It was so well received that reprints were in instant demand. In the following months, other parts of Joe also became authors, making for a whole series of articles. Joe's thymus, I thought, showed considerable literary ability. I never dreamed that a thymus could write so well. The fingers of Shakespeare wrote beautifully. But every part of Joe, it seems, breaks into national and even international print.

"I Am Joe's Pituitary Gland." "I Am Joe's Cell." "I Am Joe's Thighbone." "I Am Joe's Hair." The last article I read was written by Joe's bladder. Very interesting. What an autocrat! When he tells Joe to go, he goeth. At an important business conference, Joe's bladder speaks with greater authority than Joe's boss.

With this literary outbreak all over Joe's body, no doubt other parts of him are, even now, seated at computers in their efforts to get a piece of the action.

Me, for instance. I really don't expect millions to read what I write. I have long been accustomed to neglect. Joe's toenails receive regular attention. His smallest finger is generally washed and groomed. Even the molar deepest in his mouth and farthest from public view gets a daily scrubbing, plus expert inspection twice a year. I wish I were considered that important. I ought to be, for actually, nothing is more significant about Joe than me.

I am Joe's soul. I am undervalued by so many, but without me, Joe just isn't Joe. True, I have never been isolated in a laboratory. You cannot see me as you can Joe's nose. But to question my reality on the basis of my invisibility would be as wrong as the belief that Joe is merely the sum of his physical parts. He isn't. There is a significant difference between Joe and his dog. I am that difference.

That makes me very valuable. Joe's heart, kidneys, lungs, and blood are all intricate and marvelous and valuable. As the Bible says, he is "fearfully and wonderfully made." Yet, without belittling any one of them, I must say that I am of more worth than all of them together. Nicholas Berdyaev said, "In a certain sense, every single human soul has more meaning and value than the whole of history with its empires, its wars and revolutions, its blossoming and fading civilizations." Jesus Christ said it even better when he asked, "What good is it for a man to gain the whole world, yet forfeit his soul?"

That last quotation indicates that I am not only valuable, but losable. This requires a brief explanation. Joe can lose me. But when he does, it is not at all like losing his leg. When Joe loses his hair, it is gone. When Joe has an appendectomy, he is minus his appendix. When Joe gets careless with a saw, he is separated from his finger. But when he loses me, we are still together. I know this sounds illogical and confusing; neverthe-less it is the truth. Perhaps it is made more understandable when I explain that "losing me" really means turning me over to Satan.

May I try again? When Joe loses his blood, a coroner pro-nounces him physically dead. When Joe loses me, someone higher than all of us pronounces him spiritually dead. Being such is the same as being in the devil's possession. Both of these ideas are covered with the expression "losing your soul."

If you want to hear more about all of this, ask a good spiritual doctor; there are many around. They are called *pastors*.

You can see that it is important that Joe be constantly con-cerned about my state of well-being, especially since I lack the recuperative powers contained in Joe's physical makeup.

When Joe's body gets sick, for example, a whole army in his blood is activated to fight the disease. If a splinter works into his finger, that army will seek to neutralize, if not expel, the foreign intruder. When Joe's body grows weary, he lays it down, and while he sleeps, the broken-down cells rebuild them-selves. This power of renewal, cleansing, and rebuilding, resi-dent within Joe's body, is not in me. You have heard the expres-sion, "Physician, heal thyself." A soul cannot do that. Whether I get sick or die, wander or get lost, Joe needs a higher power to keep me well and strong.

But I must end. "What good is it for a man to gain the whole world, yet forfeit his soul?" He who asked that question also asked another. "What will a man give for his soul?" He did not ask, "What will a man take for his soul?" because he knew how very little men will take for me. A mess of pottage! A fleshpot in Egypt! A fleeting moment's fleeting honor! An illegitimate pleasure! A few more years on earth!

Pathetic!

But what will a man give for his soul? After he has lost it! Neglected it! What can he give? Tears forever flowing? All the labor of his hands? Remorse? Prayers and gifts and money and sacrifice?

I am Joe's soul. When I am well and healthy and joyful and free, it is because of something that happened two thousand years ago. A bloodied cross. An emptied tomb.

Indeed, when I am well and healthy and joyful and free, I hear Joe singing. He sings: "Love so amazing, so divine, demands my life, my soul, . . ."

selective hearing

Chapter Forty-Five

They were a couple in their seventies. She had asked for some help. He had not budged from his chair. He was a little deaf. I had stopped by for a quick "hello" and found them quarreling. "But I didn't hear you," he said. She turned to me. "He has selective hearing, you know."

I thought about it on the way home. I supposed that most people have selective hearing.

The Reverend Doctor Dryce Herman ascended his pulpit. He had chosen his text carefully from one of the apocryphal books: *The Versifications of Mother Goose.* The Sunday morning bulletin repeated his sermon title, which had been announced in the *Saturday Evening Press:* "The Hubbard Cubbard." He preferred his own spelling to "cupboard." Conforming it to "Hubbard" made it look better in print. He read the text slowly and solemnly:

Old Mother Hubbard went to the cupboard
To get her poor dog a bone.
When she got there, the cupboard was bare,
And so the poor dog had none.

Repeating the last line for effect, the Reverend Doctor Dryce Herman launched his message: "My dear friends: I bring you a very important message today. The theme this morning is 'The Hubbard Cubbard.' I wish to call your attention, in the first place, to its assuring presence. In the second place, I direct your thinking to its hopeful promise. And in the third and final place, I wish to focus your minds and hearts upon its empty provision and its ultimate paradox." (The last point was really two points, but he combined them. Three points were a tradition in his church.) In the conclusion and "application," he dwelt on that empty cupboard as a pretense, a prank, a parody, a prevarication. He loved alliteration.

After church, Manny A. Day went home to his convalescent wife. They had been married fifty years. "Tell me about the sermon," she said. "It was all about old age," he replied. "The minister said a lot of things. He said, 'Mother Hubbard was really old. We don't know exactly how old, but she wasn't young. She had acquired a few possessions in her years: a dog, a cupboard, and maybe some more. In spite of her age, she was able to move around quite a bit. A blessing. She could walk to the cupboard. And she wasn't lazy. She didn't send her husband or her children. She went herself. Commendable. But, like most older folk, she too had experienced some disappointments in life. Her cupboard was bare.'"

Percy Verance said grace at the table that Sunday afternoon. He was married with five children. He was a self-made man. Starting from scratch, he had built himself quite a business. He had overcome the hardships. He had "hung in there," as he said so often. During the meal he talked. "Fine sermon this morning. I hope you children listened well. And I hope you will always remember those key words of the text: 'when she got there.' She went! And she got there! So many just don't get there. They set out for one thing, but end up somewhere else, or even nowhere. But that old lady Hubbard was something. She veered neither to the left nor to the right. She did not allow herself to be enticed. Nor diverted. No distractions. No digressions. No sirree! Her concentration was unbroken! She set herself a goal, and she made it. Are you listening?"

"Yes, Dad."

I. M. Poor had hoped for an invitation to a Sunday dinner from one of the church families, but no one asked. Maybe next week. At home, and in his little kitchen, he nibbled at his meager fare and thought about the sermon. A good message. It had really come to grips with the problem of poverty. That empty cupboard was really a symbol. The point was that there were far too many empty cupboards around, and what can we do about them? For one thing, we need more Hubbards. She didn't have a bone to share. But if she had one, she would give it away. Like St. Francis, she wouldn't rest so long as there was one hungry dog in all the land.

That week the Reverend Doctor Dryce Herman received appreciative notes from a few members: Manny, Percy, and that Poor fellow. All had enjoyed the message. He smiled and thought, "Apparently Dryce Herman didn't have a dry sermon." From their remarks, however, it seemed that all had heard a different message. Had they been in his church or elsewhere? Jesus said, "He who has ears, let him hear" (Matt. 11:15). He also said, "Consider carefully how you listen" (Luke 8:18) and "what you hear" (Mark 4:24). He did not approve of selective hearing.

At the grocery store that afternoon, the Reverend Doctor Dryce Herman met Mrs. Uppity, carrying her manicured poodle. She too said that she had enjoyed the sermon on "Kindness

to Animals." The minister raised his eyebrows. "Just think!"
she added, remembering the sermon: "No bone!"

"That poor dog!"

mutual admiration society

Chapter Forty-Six

"The offering will now be received." The organist began to play something by Bach as the minister, having announced the collection, sat down in the big pulpit chair. The deacons marched forward down the center and side aisles. It was a weekly ritual during which some in the congregation turned their thoughts inward and some outward.

Among the latter was the middle-aged woman in the back pew. With her walking difficulty, the last row was the most easily accessible. She had taken to it ever since she had taken to a cane. As the deacons moved forward, her eyes rested on the one on the left. She did not know him very well, for their congregation was large. But a year ago he had called on her to ask if she needed any help. She had served him a cup of coffee as they visited and, before he left, he had offered a prayer. She had never had such a visit from a deacon before. Since that day, she always looked for him in church and watched him as he passed the plate. What a fine young man he was! She was old enough to be his mother, and she wished she was. Her neighbor lady had said only the past week that the younger generation was a problem. That was an overgeneralization. Her young deacon friend was as fine a young man as you'd ever want to meet. A sincere Christian! She thanked the Lord for him and others like him as she fished in her purse for her mite.

The young deacon, unaware of the kind eyes that followed him from the back row, took the plate from the white-maned gentleman who had sat in the same place for as long as the deacon could remember. That old man experienced a lot since his hair had been dark, when he had been the leader in the Boys Club and his teacher in the church school. He had always been, and still was, fairly wealthy. He had lived a busy life. But church had always come first with him. He had lost his wife only recently and, years ago, a son in the war. No wonder his hair was white! But he had remained firm in the faith through all the changes. A good example! Too bad he had missed serving with him on the church council. They said he'd always been a rather quiet elder, but that when he spoke it was generally worthwhile. Respectfully he took the plate from the old gentleman and handed it to the person in the pew behind.

As he did so, the white-maned patriarch, looking ahead and across the aisle, took note of the young girl in the yellow dress. He knew her parents, grandparents, and even her great-grandparents. Good stock! How old was she? It seemed as if she'd just been born yesterday, but there she was, looking all of fourteen years or so. Where did the time go? A nice girl. He liked the way she sat and sang and listened. He also liked the fact that she was involved in the church's activities. With youngsters like her coming along, the church had nothing to worry about. He'd heard that she was preparing to make profession of her faith. What would she and her generation experience?

With such great changes taking place in society—not all for the better—he wasn't so sure he envied her. But he was old and tired. He didn't agree with those who said, "What a shame that youth is wasted on the young." That's the way God put it all together, and what God did was good. He closed his eyes and sighed a prayer for the next generation and the young lady across and ahead. He thanked God for her.

Unaware that someone had said a prayer for her, the girl in the yellow dress watched the preacher. Was he nervous? She would be if she had to preach. But, she supposed, preachers got used to it. She had talked to him about making profession of her faith, so she was getting to know him a little better. He really was a nice man, and he knew the Bible. She looked at her parents and her kid brother and felt thankful for everything and everyone, including the minister who was looking out over the congregation.

The deacons were almost finished. The minister watched as they reached the last row. He saw the lady in the back shift her cane as she reached for the plate. He remembered her telephone call of a few days before. She had said she had to go to the hospital, but she wasn't worried. What a fine woman she was! Always uncomplaining and always thankful to the Lord. She was a better Christian than he was. He hoped he could grow to her spiritual maturity.

The deacons were coming forward. The collection had been received. But more had happened than the playing of Bach and the offering of tithes. From the woman in the back to the deacon, to the white-haired saint to the young girl, to the preacher and back to the woman in the rear—a full circle of appreciation had been drawn with nobody's knowledge but God's.

Critics say that a lot of bad happens in churches. They are right. There was much to reprimand in the early churches, too—read the epistles. But within the Christian fold is also a lot of good. The Lord, who in his omniscience sees the bad, also sees the good.